Elite • 154

# Vietnam Airmobile Warfare Tactics

Gordon L Rottman • Illustrated by Adam Hook

*Consultant editor* Martin Windrow

First published in Great Britain in 2007 by Osprey Publishing,
Midland House, West Way, Botley, Oxford OX2 0PH, UK
44-02 23rd St, Suite 219, Long Island City, NY 11101, USA
Email: info@ospreypublishing.com

Osprey Publishing is part of the Osprey Group.

Transferred to digital print on demand 2011

First published 2007
2nd impression 2008

Printed and bound by PrintOnDemand-Worldwide.com, Peterborough, UK

A CIP catalogue record for this book is available from the British Library

ISBN: 978 1 84603 136 6

Series Editor: Martin Windrow
Page layouts by Ken Vail Graphic Design, Cambridge, UK
Cartography by Map Studio
Index by Sharon Shotter
Originated by PPS Grasmere Ltd, Leeds, UK
Typeset in Helvetica Neue and ITC New Baskerville

### Acknowledgements
The author is indebted to Kenneth Henson (Col, US Army, Rtd) for his advice
and assistance, and to Leroy ("Red") Wilson for the loan of photographs.
   Author and publishers wish to record their gratitude to Simon Dunstan
for generous assistance with photographs.

### The Woodland Trust
Osprey Publishing is supporting the Woodland Trust, the UK's leading
woodland conservation charity, by funding the dedication of trees.

www.ospreypublishing.com

### Artist's note
Readers may care to note the original paintings from which the colour
plates in this book were prepared are available for private sale.
All reproduction copyright whatsoever is retained by the publisher.
Enquiries should be addressed to:

Scorpio Gallery, P.O. Box 475, Hailsham, E. Sussex BN27 2SL

The publishers regret that they can enter into no correspondence upon
this matter.

### Abbreviations used in this text:

| | |
|---|---|
| AbnDiv | Airborne Division |
| AH- | Attack Helicopter |
| AO | area of operations |
| ARA | aerial rocket artillery |
| ARVN | Army of the Republic of Vietnam |
| Bde | brigade |
| CavDiv | Cavalry Division |
| C&C | command and control |
| CH- | Cargo Helicopter |
| CTZ | Corps Tactical Zone |
| HMH | Marine heavy helicopter squadron |
| HML | Marine light helicopter squadron |
| HMM | Marine medium helicopter squadron |
| HQ | headquarters |
| InfDiv | Infantry Division |
| LOH | light observation helicopter |
| LRRP | long-range reconnaissance patrol |
| LZ | landing zone |
| Medevac | medical evacuation |
| NVA | North Vietnamese Army |
| OH- | Observation Helicopter |
| PZ | pick-up zone |
| VC | Viet Cong |
| VMO | Marine observation squadron |
| UH- | Utility Helicopter |

### Linear measurement
The US Armed Forces used the metric system (meters and kilometers)
for range and distance measurement, and this practice is continued in this
book. Feet and inches were used for the dimensions of aircraft, weapons,
structures, etc. From conversion from metric to US systems:
kilometers to miles = multiply kilometers by 0.6214
meters to feet = multiply meters by 3.2808
Ordinal numbers
Current styles are used in this text – e.g. 2d, 3d.

**FRONT COVER:**
**A group of infantrymen from the 1st Cavalry Division jump
from a Bell UH-1 Iroquois, also known as a "Huey", as they
begin a recconnaissance mission in Vietnam.
(Bettmann/CORBIS)**

# VIETNAM AIRMOBILE WARFARE TACTICS

## INTRODUCTION

Even though the US Army possessed the Army Air Forces during World War II, this was actually a semi-independent arm inclusive of the Army Air Corps. The Army Ground Forces had need of its own organic aviation in the form of light liaison and artillery spotter aircraft. The Army Air Forces became a separate service in 1947, with the establishment of the US Air Force. However, the Army still needed its own aircraft in the form of fixed-wing planes and helicopters, and this resulted in endless disputes between the Army and Air Force due to their overlapping requirements – an on-going quarrel lasting until 1975.

In 1947 the Army procured its first observation helicopters. Alongside light fixed-wing aircraft, their use gradually increased through the Korean War (1950–53), but numbers remained small; the Army made only limited use of helicopters for liaison, medical evacuation, artillery spotting and resupply. It was not until the mid-1950s that the procurement of helicopters, and an interest in developing new tactical techniques for their employment, both increased, giving rise to a more robust doctrine. In 1954 the Army Aviation School moved from Camp Sill, OK, to Fort Rucker, AL, and in 1955 it became the US Army Aviation Center. The next year the Primary Aviator Flight School was opened at Ft Wolters, TX. In 1956 experimentation with armed helicopters began. Development continued as Army aviation grew slowly; and in 1962 it was recommended that the airmobile concept be adopted. The aim was to provide ground units with unprecedented mobility, and the ability to fly over difficult terrain and by-pass major obstacles and enemy forces.

Army Aviation did not become a branch of the Army until 1983. During the Vietnam War aviation units and aviators were assigned to infantry, armor, artillery, transportation, medical, military intelligence and other branches. This decentralized employment of aviation assets was less than satisfactory; aviation was thought of as just another means of transportation, and was integrated into units along the lines of trucks. The official mission statement of Army aviation was, "to

A classic scene from the world's first "helicopter war": a heavily loaded scout from Company E, 2d Battalion, 5th Cavalry of the 1st Cavalry Division (Airmobile) waves in an approaching UH-1 "Huey" to land on a sandbar in the bend of a river. Given the scarcity of clearings in jungle terrain, river sandbars and beaches made valuable landing zones. (US Army, courtesy Simon Dunstan)

May 1963: at Moc Hoa airstrip, Saigon, US Army CH-21B Shawnees from 57th Transportation Company (Light Helicopter) prepare to lift ARVN troops of the 7th Marines; the marines are lined up in "sticks," prepared to board the choppers in order. Such operations had been going on in South Vietnam for more than a year, while back in the States the first cadres for the 11th Air Assault Div were only just gathering at Ft Benning. (US Army, courtesy Simon Dunstan)

augment the capability of the Army to conduct prompt and sustained combat operations on land. Army aviation accomplishes this mission by providing aviation support to Army organizations at all command levels." It is notable that the word "aviation" was not capitalized in this statement, emphasizing that it was not an entity or separate organization within the Army, but was fully integrated across that service.

The Marine Corps had long possessed its own air arm, and experienced less opposition to the development of its helicopter capabilities. The Corps quickly became concerned over the viability of amphibious operations in the face of nuclear weapons, and as early as 1946 it was suggested that helicopters could be employed to exploit the "vertical flank" rather than presenting the enemy with an amphibious force as a target. The Corps' first experimental helicopter unit was commissioned at the end of 1947. The Marines deployed helicopter units to Korea, and increased their use in 1951; they made more aggressive use of helicopters, employing them for scouting, command and control, resupply and medical evacuation, and also conducting the first modest troop lifts. Marine helicopter units continued to expand after the Korean War, and the first amphibious assault ship – effectively a troop and helicopter transport – was commissioned in 1956.

Despite this slow start, by the early 1960s the relevance of helicopters to the situation developing in South Vietnam was certainly recognized. The American-supported government of the Republic of Vietnam was increasingly harried by the expanding operations of the Viet Cong (VC) insurgents, supported by the funneling from communist North Vietnam of first material aid, and then North Vietnamese Army (NVA) troops. It was fully recognized that helicopters were extremely valuable for lifting troops, resupply, medical evacuation, command and control, liaison, scouting and target spotting, and their potential for fire support was beginning to be realized. Besides advisors, among the first Army and Marine personnel to deploy to Vietnam were helicopter units.

The Army deployed two light helicopter companies to Vietnam at the end of 1961, and the first airmobile assault operations with Army of the Republic of Vietnam (ARVN) troops were conducted on January 2, 1962. An experimental attack helicopter unit also arrived in 1961, and three more transport companies deployed. In April, the first Marine medium helicopter squadron arrived in country, together with an Army medical evacuation (medevac) detachment. These units were deployed throughout the country to provide airmobile support to ARVN units in each of the four corps tactical zones (CTZ).[1] The Marine squadron rotated every six months and operated in the far north of South Vietnam, since its helicopters were better suited for higher altitudes. Army units were increased, with 200 aircraft in operation by the end of 1962. When Army and Marine combat units began arriving in Vietnam in early 1965, the number of aviation units expanded greatly.

These were not the first helicopters to see service in Vietnam, but they were the first to be employed for lifting troops into action. The French had received a trickle of light helicopters in Indochina in 1950–54, but at their peak these only reached a total of between two and three dozen – an insignificant number compared to the thousands later employed by the US forces – and these were employed almost exclusively for casualty evacuation.[2]

Those early US efforts prior to 1965 had developed many of the basic tactics and techniques used in Vietnam; the units involved had experienced the extremes of climate, assessed the enemy threat, and provided valuable lessons for the Army Aviation Center and Marines. There was still much to learn, but those early pioneering units had broken a great deal of ground.

# THE HELICOPTER

Helicopter design was constantly evolving throughout the war. Completely new models were being fielded by the time US combat units arrived in 1965; modifications and improvements were repeatedly made to existing models, and experimentation with weapons systems was a non-stop process.

Prior to September 18, 1962, different aircraft designation systems were used by the different services. On that date the Air Force's 1948 system was adopted by all services, resulting in the redesignation of Army and Marine helicopters. The basic categories included: attack helicopter (AH), cargo helicopter (CH), observation helicopter (OH), and utility helicopter (UH). Series modifications were identified by the letters "A" on upwards. Modifications invariably meant increased or improved engine power, endurance, avionics and crew accommodations.

---

[1] The Army 8th, 57th, 93d, 33d, and 81st Transportation Companies (Light Helicopter) each had 20x H-21B (later CH-21B) cargo helicopters. The 57th Medical Detachment (Helicopter Ambulance) had 5x HU-1A (later designated UH-1A) utility helicopters. The Marine HMM-362 had 12x HUS-1 (later CH-34D) medium helicopters. The attack unit – Utility Tactical Transport Helicopter Company (later 68th Aviation Company) – had HU-1A gunships. In July 1961, the Army deployed the 45th Transportation Battalion (Transport Aircraft) to control these helicopter units.

[2] It was not until their return to the Algerian War, which broke out in 1954, that the French began serious experiments with troop lifts, but such operations became commonplace from mid-1956 when they received the Vertol CH-21. The British also employed 20 to 30 Sikorsky S-55s in Malaya in 1950–60, for a range of counterinsurgency missions including, from spring 1953, regular troop insertions. A helicopter assault landing was made by Royal Marines of 45 Commando at Port Said, Egypt, during the Anglo-French Suez operation of November 6, 1956.

It took little imagination to give the nickname of "Flying Banana" to the Boeing Vertol CH-21B, here carrying a 105mm M101A1 howitzer as a sling load. While the Huey replaced the CH-21B as the main troop lift type, it was unable to sling a 105mm.

Army helicopter types were officially named after Indian tribes; Marine and Navy helicopter names usually featured the prefix "Sea-." Numerous slang terms, aside from these official names, were used to identify the different types of helicopters (collectively, "choppers, birds, ships, helios" – the last mainly used by the Marines) in terms of their missions. Attack helicopters were "gunships"; UH-1 utility helicopters carrying troops were called "slicks," or occasionally "school buses." AH-1 Cobra attack helicopters were differentiated from UH-1B/C gunships by the terms "Snakes" and "Hogs" respectively. "Heavy Hog" also referred to gunships with the maximum load of rocket pods, including Cobras – loaded that heavily, they handled like a hog. A UH-1C gunship with a chin turret grenade-launcher was sometimes called a "Frog." Light observation helicopters (LOH) were collectively known as "Loaches," although this name was mainly associated with the OH-6 Cayuse. Command-and-control choppers were simply called "C&C," "Charlie-Charlie" or "Chuck-Chuck"; these had a console in the troop compartment with several radios and a secure voice device. Medical evacuation (medevac) choppers were called "Dust-Offs," after the radio call sign of the first such unit.

Only the most commonly used helicopter types are listed below, simply to provide a basis of understanding of their roles and capabilities. The passenger capacities quoted here for each type are the design loads, but they were lower in actual practice. Most choppers had a crew of four: two pilots (the senior designated the aircraft commander), a crew chief and a

March 1968: loading a Bell UH-1D from the 191st AHC ("Boomerangs") with 81mm mortar ammunition, C-rations and 5gal plastic water bags for delivery to isolated company bases of the 199th Inf Bde, defending the southern approaches to Saigon. (US Army, courtesy Simon Dunstan)

gunner – the crew chief also doubled as a door gunner. In most armed helicopters the co-pilot usually operated the weapons; Cobras had two pilots seated in tandem, with the co-pilot forward. Observation helicopters had only one pilot and a crew chief/observer.

The first **ARMY** helicopter type deployed to Vietnam was the Boeing Vertol CH-21B Shawnee cargo helicopter, the "Flying Banana" or "Hog Two-One." It could carry 22 troops, and was armed only with a .30cal machine gun in the left troop door – the right side pilot usually carried a submachine gun in an attempt to protect that side. The CH-21B/C was replaced by the UH-1 in 1963/64.

The heavy lift helicopter was the Sikorsky CH-37B Mojave, used by both the Army (H-37) and Marines (HR2S or "Deuce"). It could carry two jeeps or a 105mm howitzer or 26 troops. In Vietnam it was mainly used for recovering downed helicopters and other heavy lift missions. By 1965 it was being replaced by the Army's CH-47A and CH-54A, and in the Marines by the CH-53A.

By far the most widely used helicopter was the Bell UH-1 Iroquois series, universally known as the "Huey" (it had originally been designated HU-1A). It was initially planned as a medevac chopper, but was then found to be an excellent troop-lifter even though it carried only six passengers. The UH-1Bs saw early use as troop-lifters, but they mostly served as gunships and utility/liaison choppers. The UH-1C, introduced in 1965, was provided with a more powerful engine and was intended as a gunship. Armament varied widely, but might include two forward-firing 7.62mm machine guns on both sides, two side-firing door guns, combinations of rocket pods, and often a 40mm grenade-launcher in a chin turret. Aerial rocket artillery (ARA) UH-1B/Cs had only two 24-tube rocket pods and door guns. The UH-1D, introduced in 1963, was a "stretched" version able to carry up to 11 troops and with more powerful engines; the UH-1H appeared in late 1967 with an even more powerful engine. More than 2,000 UH-1Ds and almost 3,600 UH-1Hs were procured; the armament of these slicks was two 7.62mm M60D door guns.

The Bell AH-1G Cobra (formally named the Huey Cobra, rather than after an Indian tribe, but the name never took) became the standard gunship in 1967; in that year it began replacing the Huey Hogs, although

This CH-54A Tarhe from the 478th Avn Co (Heavy Helicopter), attached to 159th Avn Bn (Assault Helicopter) of 101st Abn Div (Airmobile), is lifting an M450 Mini-Dozer into a fire support base in 1971. The aircraft's "buzz number" has been painted in white beside the original black number, to allow air traffic control to identify it for radio communication. (US Army, courtesy Simon Dunstan)

those remained in use for some time. The state-of-the-art Cobra set a new world standard for attack helicopters; it was fast, streamlined, and well armed with a 40mm grenade-launcher, a 7.62mm minigun and rocket pods. At the end of the war a three-barrel rotary 20mm cannon was mounted in the chin turret. From mid-1970 the Marines used some AH-1G Cobras; in 1971 these were augmented by a few AH-1J Sea Cobras with twin engines and a three-barrel 20mm cannon.[3]

The first observation helicopter deployed to Vietnam was the Bell OH-13G/H/S Sioux, dating from the Korean War as the H-13. This little bubble-canopy scout was entirely inadequate; while it could carry two passengers like later scouts, its only crew was the pilot, and armament was two machine guns mounted on the skids. The similar Hiller OH-23G Raven saw comparable use; but both were replaced in early 1968 with the Hughes OH-6A Cayuse. This had significantly increased speed, lift and endurance, and was considered one of the most crash-survivable helicopters in the inventory. It usually mounted a 7.62mm minigun; an M60D was sometimes mounted in the right or left rear door. It began to be partly replaced by the Bell OH-58A Kiowa, mounting similar armament, in 1969.

The twin-rotor Boeing Vertol CH-47A Chinook ("Shithook" or "Forty-Seven") was a medium cargo helicopter for transporting troops, artillery, ammunition and light vehicles (jeeps or Mechanical Mules). It could sling-load a 105mm howitzer, or carry 33 troops. First deployed to Vietnam in 1965, the A-model began to be replaced with the CH-47B in 1967; the CH-47A had proved to be underpowered, with a disappointing lift capacity and range, and also experienced such extreme mechanical problems that often a unit could only put 50 percent in the air. The CH-47B was also inadequate, and the CH-47C began arriving in 1968.

[3] See Osprey Combat Aircraft 41, *US Army AH-1 Cobra Units in Vietnam*; New Vanguard 87, *Bell UH-1 Huey "Slicks" 1962–75*; and NVG 125, *Huey Cobra Gunships*.

The Sikorsky CH-54A Tarhe or "Flying Crane" was a massive heavy lift helicopter. It could lift a 155mm howitzer, or a van-like "people pod" taking 45 troops and was also capable of being fitted out as a command post or an emergency operating room. These were little used, however; and while the CH-54A's primary role was to recover aircraft, it was also used to move anything from river patrol boats to bridge sections.

The **MARINE CORPS** initially used the Sikorsky HUS-1 ("Huss"), later redesignated the UH-34D Seahorse ("Dog"). The Army called this the CH-34 Choctaw, but did not send it to Vietnam. The UH-34D carried 18 troops and was initially unarmed, but a gun was soon mounted in the right door, to be followed by another in the left troop compartment window. The UH-34D was phased out by mid-1969.

CH-47 Chinook medium cargo helicopter lifting construction materials into a recently established fire support base – many FSBs in remote and roadless areas could only be established and supplied by helicopter. At left is a 155mm M114A1 howitzer. (Leroy "Red" Wilson)

The Hughes OH-6A Cayuse – universally called the "Loach" in a corruption of LOH, "light observation helicopter." This example bears full Stateside colors, including the white ARMY, full-color national insignia, yellow aircraft numbers and tail rotor caution band.

Little used in Vietnam, the "people pod" fitted beneath a CH-54A could carry 45 troops or 24 litters. They were also used as mobile command posts; and in the medical role, fitted out as emergency operating rooms, they could be delivered to a firebase, detached, and could immediately begin operations on casualties.

In 1966 the Boeing Vertol CH-46A Sea Knight or "Phrog" (it looked like a frog ready to hop) began replacing the "Huss" to become the Marines' principal troop and medium cargo helicopter. Looking somewhat like a scaled-down Chinook, this carried 22 troops. Many were armed with two .50cal machine guns, but these could not be dismounted if the helicopter was downed, so some crews preferred M60s. The CH-46A suffered numerous problems, and the much improved CH-46D arrived in Vietnam at the end of 1967.

To replace the CH-37B Mojave, the Sikorsky CH-53A Sea Stallion or "Buff" (for "big ugly fellow," or something similar) was introduced in 1966 as the Marines' new heavy lift cargo chopper. This could carry 38 troops or a large amount of cargo, and could sling-load a 155mm howitzer or an Ontos antitank vehicle.

Riggers detach a sling load of C-rations from a CH-46A Sea Knight; the subdued marking "HMM-364" identifies Marine Medium Helicopter Squadron 364. Note the .50cal MG mounted in the side window. At left, a radio operator with an AN/PRC-25 communicates with the aircrew; at right, the ground guide is signaling "hold." (US Marines, courtesy Simon Dunstan)

The carcass of a UH-1D rests on an AMMI barge after recovery from a river. Even when un-rebuildable, downed helicopters were recovered to be cannibalized for scarce spare parts, and to deny the enemy propaganda photographs. The peak year for losses was 1969, with 459 lost to enemy action and 598 to other causes, during 8,441,000 sorties by almost 3,400 helicopters. (That was the peak number serving at any one time; more than 1,000 others served as replacements.) On average, therefore, only one helicopter was shot down per 20,600 sorties, and one hit per 1,300 sorties. (Leroy "Red" Wilson)

The Marine version of the Huey was the UH-1E, a modified UH-1B. The Corps used it mainly as a utility, liaison and rescue aircraft (it was equipped with a hoist), and troop lift was secondary. Only 250 of these machines were procured. Some were armed for the gunship role with twin 7.62mm machine guns on the sides, rocket pods, and a pair of machine guns in a chin turret.

## The enemy threat to helicopters

Helicopters were relatively slow, lightly armored and fragile. Many felt that they would be highly vulnerable to light antiaircraft and small arms fire. The nature of their operations often required them to fly low, and they would have to land in enemy-controlled territory to deliver troops and supplies; this obviously increased their vulnerability, and it was widely anticipated that losses would be high.

Some 12,000 helicopters of all services were sent to Vietnam; from 1961 to 1971, the US forces lost 2,066 helicopters to enemy action, and another 2,566 to operational accidents, mishaps and weather. More than 22,000 helicopters were hit, many of them more than once. This might be considered high – but the context was more than 36 million sorties flown during this period.

Most of the weather mishaps were due to heavy rain, fog or low cloud when visual contact with the ground was lost. Most helicopters were equipped to fly with instrument flight rules (IFR), but few airfields were equipped with instrument approach systems. The major problem was that pilots had little experience with IFR even though they were rated with either a Standard or Tactical Instrument Ticket. To maintain IFR proficiency required a great deal of time, which was not available, and was extremely difficult. Additionally, there were usually insufficient on-board fuel reserves to fly IFR.

In order to maximize helicopter lift capacity and maneuverability the machines could only be provided with limited armor. Only pilots were provided with armored seats, offering protection from below, the rear, and (partially) from the outboard sides. The engine compressor was partly protected by armor, but the highly vulnerable tail rotor gearboxes

**11**

The Soviet-made 12.7mm DShKM38/46 heavy machine gun, and its Chinese-made Type 54 copy, was the principal antiaircraft weapon fielded by the VC/NVA; it was effective from 800–1,200m, and had a 540–600rpm rate of fire. American troops knew it as the ".51cal."

and transmission were not. Fire extinguishers were carried, but there was no engine compartment fire suppression system, merely infrared fire detectors to set off warning lights. All crewmen wore body armor vests, and the aviator's helmet offered some ballistic protection. Vests were provided with add-on front and back "chicken plates," but the back plate was often discarded. Fire-resistant flight suits and gloves were used, and canvas-topped jungle boots were given up for all-leather boots offering better fire protection. Gunners would sometimes sit on spare armor vests or scrounged armor plate, but most enemy fire came from the sides.

The safest altitudes to fly were either very low or very high. High speed, treetop-level flight (below 100 feet) made it extremely difficult for a gunner on the ground to hit a helicopter. It was hard to determine the exact direction it was coming from, and the noise was not heard as early as when it was flying higher; the aircraft came over so fast and low that it was only exposed for seconds. Another method was "nape-of-the earth" flight; this technique entailed the helicopter flying over and among trees and terrain features, using them as cover and constantly varying altitude and speed. From beneath double-canopy forests and rubber trees it was virtually impossible to see a helicopter, or for it to see the ground. To avoid antiaircraft fire a safe altitude was 1,000–1,500ft, and high altitude flight also improved radio range.

The most vulnerable time for a helicopter was when it was transiting from forward flight to ground-effect just as it was landing. It was moving forward very slowly at this point, and would require valuable moments to transition to take-off. Of course, hovering just above or actually sitting on the ground made it a stationary target, even though it would only take seconds to off-load its troops. A helicopter taking off under fire was also in serious danger, since it was low, the speed could only build up gradually, and the pilot could not take evasive maneuvers because of other helicopters on and around the LZ, and had to avoid trees. Attack helicopters were vulnerable when making their run on the target, since the enemy knew that they had to fly on a straight course in a shallow dive.

To reduce enemy fire on potentially hot LZs, these would be generously "prepped" by artillery followed by gunships. The lift helicopters would suppress the treeline with their machine guns, before off-loading and departing in seconds. A significant problem was simply that unless aircrews detected muzzle flashes or tracers, or felt the impact of hits, they did not know they were under fire. Sometimes other aircraft notified them, and experimental gunfire detectors were installed on a few aircraft; but for the most part crews did not know they were taking fire until they heard disturbing noises actually in the fabric of their helicopters.

The VC/NVA were well equipped with automatic weapons. The semi-automatic SKS carbine and selective fire AK-47 and AKM assault rifles fired a small but deadly 7.62mm round and were effective against

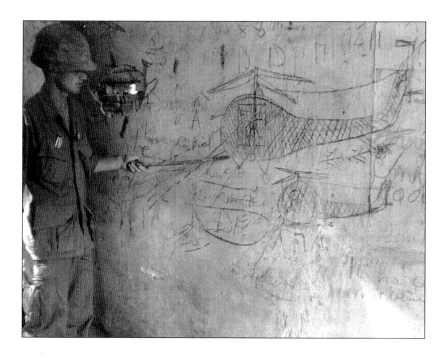

August 1967: a VC training aid, showing techniques for shooting at helicopters with small arms, found by 2/11th Armd Cav on the wall of an abandoned house southwest of Chu Lai during Operation "Hood River." (US Army, courtesy Simon Dunstan)

aircraft within a few hundred meters, although captured US 5.56mm M16A1 rifles had only limited effect. The Soviet bloc 7.62mm machine guns, as well as captured 7.62mm and .30cal guns, were effective up to 500–600 meters against moving aircraft. The VC/NVA were taught to lead aircraft based on the angle of approach and airspeed, and to fire into the engines and pilot compartments of landing, landed or departing helicopters.

A major consideration for the employment of antiaircraft weapons was effective camouflage. The goal was to "ambush" helicopters at close range with massed weapons from multiple directions. Once helicopters located antiaircraft positions the gunners were trained to withdraw.

May 1968: a Marine CH-46A Sea Knight burns on an LZ after attempting to pick up wounded from Co D, 1/3d Marines; a second "Phrog" lands at high speed to extract the troops and aircrew survivors. (US Marine Corps, courtesy Simon Dunstan)

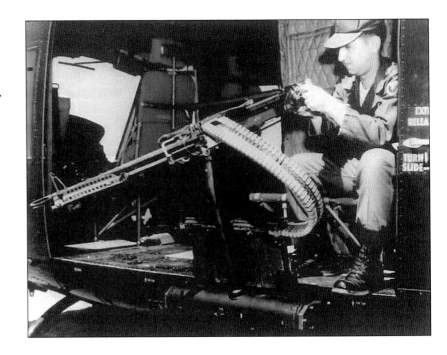

A door gunner, here not wearing normal flight gear, demonstrates a 7.62mm M60D door gun on a pedestal mount – the XM23 armament subsystem. Note the 500-round ammunition container and the flexible feed chute – the latter was often discarded.

Pamphlets were distributed outlining antihelicopter tactics. Cardboard silhouettes were suspended from cords between trees, and gunners practiced proper tracking and leading. The VC/NVA placed such a high priority on knocking down helicopters that they would continue to fire on departing aircraft rather than on the troops they had inserted, even though these presented an immediate threat. Being credited with a helicopter kill was a great honor.

The most deadly weapon employed by the enemy was the Soviet 12.7mm DShKM38/46 machine gun, which aviators called the ".51 caliber."[4] While heavy and bulky, it could be man-packed through the jungle, and was provided with a high tripod and antiaircraft sights. Its standard ammunition was armor-piercing/incendiary, deadly to aircraft. Captured US .50cal M2 machine guns were also employed, but anti-aircraft mounts for them had to be jury-rigged. The 12.7mm guns were often employed in platoons of three.

The Soviet-made RPG-2 and RPG-7 rocket-propelled grenade-launchers – called the B-40 and B-41 by the VC/NVA – were frequently used against helicopters, and a hit by one of these 85mm shaped charge warheads was usually fatal to an aircraft. If it did not strike a target the RPG-7's warhead self-destructed approximately 4.5 seconds after firing (i.e. after traveling about 920 meters or 1,006yds), and this characteristic was sometimes exploited in an effort to achieve an airburst near a helicopter. More realistically, the RPG was effective against a stationary target at 500 meters and slow-moving targets at 300 meters.

Only limited use was made of the Soviet 37mm M1939 (Chinese Type 55) antiaircraft gun, usually encountered in the north. If employed against LZs, 60mm and 81mm/82mm mortars were effective against helicopters because of their considerable fragmentation effect. The

---

[4] It was said that the DShKM38/46 could fire US .50cal ammunition, but not vice versa; this is untrue. While both were actually .511cal, neither weapon could fire the other's ammunition – the cartridge case dimensions were significantly different.

Soviet shoulder-fired, heat-seeking SA-7 Strela surface-to-air missile was not encountered until 1972, and then only in limited numbers. They were marginally effective if the helicopter was at altitude, but aircraft that kept low and fast over the treetops could not be engaged. Helicopters were modified to vent exhaust heat into the rotor-wash to hamper the missile's heat-seeker from locking on.

In rare instances potential LZs were mined, sometimes with command-detonated munitions, at other times with above-ground tripwires on which the helicopter might sit. There was also use of booby-trap grenades: cardboard sheets or palm fronds were attached with cords to the arming pins, to be blown away by the rotor-wash of a landing helicopter. One of the most effective techniques was simply to post lookouts – often local village boys – at possible LZs to notify VC/NVA units of the approach of helicopters.

## Helicopter armament

In 1961, while reading George Orwell's classic dystopian novel *Nineteen Eighty-Four*, the present author was intrigued by Orwell's prediction of "fighter helicopters," especially since the book was written in 1948 when helicopters were barely off the ground. The author mentioned the idea to friends; thinking only of the fragile little bubble-nose helicopter in the 1957–59 television series, *Whirlybirds*, they were skeptical.

At that time the Army had recently completed the Rogers Board to study the future needs and direction of its fledgling aviation effort. While the requirements for scout and troop lift helicopters were addressed, there was such limited information regarding the idea of armed attack helicopters that the Board directed that a study be undertaken to determine "whether the concept of air fighting units was practical." Just eight years later the present author would be directing the fires of very practical Cobra gunships into a treeline.

Helicopters were armed with machine guns, cannons, automatic grenade-launchers and rockets. They could deliver an astounding

This UH-1H mounts the Firefly armament system, with a 20,000-watt Nightsun FX150 spotlight and a six-barrel 7.62mm XM134 "minigun" with a 2,000-round ammo container. During Nighthawk missions the Huey would fly low and slow to draw fire, then illuminate and open fire on the target, at which point higher flying Cobras would roll in.

The XM28E1 armament subsystem was a chin turret for the AH-1G Cobra, mounting a 7.62mm XM134 minigun and a 40mm M129 automatic grenade-launcher. The weapon positions could be switched around, or two of the same weapon mounted instead. The drum compartment for 40mm ammunition is shown here in the open position.

amount of firepower from a most appealing vantage point, and they could get that firepower to where it was needed in a short time. Besides offensive weapons, they also mounted defensive armament.

There were an almost endless number of different types of weapons mountings, called "armament subsystems." Many experimental mounts were fitted and widely used even though they had not been standardized. Weapon mountings included door and port pedestal mounts, twin gun mounts on the sides of helicopters, combination mountings of machine guns and rocket pods, chin turrets, and more.

Early door guns were standard 7.62mm M60 belt-fed machine guns with a firing rate of 600rpm, fitted to a pedestal mount or hung on bungee cords. These were "spray and pray" weapons, lacking accuracy beyond a few hundred meters: range estimation is difficult from a moving helicopter with a downward angle of fire. The M60C was a fixed gun on external forward-firing mounts, so lacking the butt stock, pistol grip/trigger group and bipod of the ground gun; it was remotely charged and fired using a solenoid. Many crew chiefs carried a trigger group so that they could dismount an M60C and fire it hand-held. The M60D also had its butt and trigger group removed, but retained the bipod; it was fitted as a door gun, and provided with spade grips and trigger with a linkage to the firing mechanism, and if necessary it could be dismounted and fired as a ground weapon.

Another 7.62mm weapon was the M134 minigun, an electrically operated, six-barrel rotary gun ("Gatling"). It had two rates of fire, 2,000 and 4,000 rpm, the former being more practical. From 1964 this weapon began replacing the twin M60Cs side-mounted on Huey gunships, and it was later mounted in the chin turret of many Cobras. Every fifth round was a tracer, and even at the lower rate of fire these appeared as a continuous red streak. However, the M134 jammed frequently owing to feed problems.

The Browning .50cal machine gun was used in some applications to provide longer range, but its real value was its penetration through dense brush, bamboo and light field fortifications. Three versions saw use: the ground M2 firing at 450–550rpm, the aircraft

M2 with a rate of 750–850rpm, and the aircraft M3, which fired at 1,150–1,250rpm. Several models of 20mm automatic cannons also saw some use, but these were found to be overly heavy and prone to malfunctions. They did have the advantage of being able to slug it out with enemy .51cals at a safe range, however.

A more effective weapon firing high explosive rounds was the 40mm automatic grenade-launcher or "thumper." The M75 in a chin turret was used on the UH-1B and early AH-1G gunships, firing at 215–230rpm. The improved M129, with a rate of 400rpm, was mounted on later AH-1Gs. These were belt-fed weapons firing higher velocity rounds than could be fired from the hand-held M79 grenade-launcher. Although called "high velocity" in comparison to the M79's low velocity rounds, they were still slow, and were not very accurate; the gunship had to be stable when firing, or the rounds went astray if fired off axis. However, these grenade-launchers were mechanically reliable.

Heavy firepower was provided in the form of the 2.75in (70mm) folding fin aircraft rocket (FFAR). These rockets had a maximum range of 8,000 meters, but their accurate range was not much over 1,000 meters; in practice they were typically launched at a slant range of 500–1,000 meters, although they could be fired at longer ranges for suppressive fire so long as there were no friendly troops near the target. There were two HE warheads, 10lb and 17lb, roughly equating in effect to 75mm and 105mm howitzer rounds; the 10lb had up to a 50-meter casualty radius. White phosphorous rounds were used for target marking and incendiary purposes. The anti-personnel flechette rocket was deadly to troops in the open: it would burst just short of the target area to shower it with 1,180 hardened steel darts.

The impact area of the rockets was controlled by the steepness of the angle of attack, and their spread by the range at which they were fired. There was a puff of red smoke at the point of detonation, but the pilot could not see the actual impact of the flechette rounds. All these rockets were launched from pods containing 7, 19, or 24 tubes, and were usually fired two at a time. A problem was encountered with rapid tube wear-out because of the heavier than expected use of 17lb warheads.

The weight of weapons, ammunition, armor and gunners meant that something had to be given up to compensate, both by the UH-1 series Huey gunships and the Cobra. Fuel had to be reduced, and less than optimum fuel/ammunition loads had to be carried on missions requiring longer ranges or longer loiter time over the target. Even with less than full fuel and ammunition loads the gunships were still heavier than the lift ships they were supporting; they could not always dash ahead to prep LZs, and might be left behind when the empty lift ships departed. If opposition was heavy on an LZ, the gunships might run out of ammunition too soon. A Cobra carrying two each 7x and 19x rocket pods and a full load of 40mm and 7.62mm ammunition could take on

The XM34 subsystem – a 20mm M24A1 cannon and a 19-tube XM159 2.75in rocket launcher – mounted on one of the four AHC-47A Chinook gunships; above, a hand-held .50cal MG is mounted in a side port – the XM32 subsystem. These rockets have 17lb warheads; the 10lb warheads did not protrude from the tubes.

The armament of the ACH-47A Chinook; with 7.62mm and .50cal machine guns, 20mm cannons, a 40mm grenade-launcher and rocket pods, they carried more firepower than a rifle company, but they were large, slow targets, and vulnerable owing to their hydraulic system.

The four aircraft were named "Cost of Living," "Easy Money," "Stump Jumper" and "Birth Control." Three served from June to October 1966 as 53d Aviation Detachment, supporting US and Australian units and, from September, 1st CavDiv, with which they stayed as 1st Avn Det (Provisional), under 228th Air Support Helicopter Battalion. One was lost in a take-off accident in August 1966, and was replaced in September; another was destroyed, killing its whole crew, in May 1967, when a 20mm mounting failed and the gun shot off the forward rotor. The remaining two "Go-Go Birds" fought on until the Tet Offensive of February 1968, when one was brought down at Hue; the lone survivor was then withdrawn.

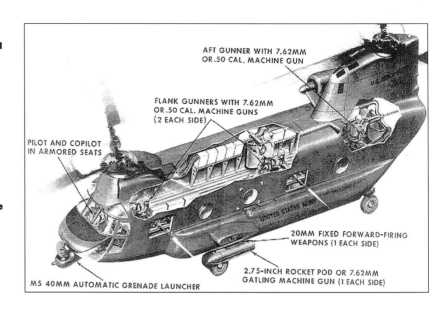

AFT GUNNER WITH 7.62MM OR .50 CAL. MACHINE GUN

FLANK GUNNERS WITH 7.62MM OR .50 CAL. MACHINE GUNS (2 EACH SIDE)

PILOT AND COPILOT IN ARMORED SEATS

20MM FIXED FORWARD-FIRING WEAPONS (1 EACH SIDE)

M5 40MM AUTOMATIC GRENADE LAUNCHER

2.75-INCH ROCKET POD OR 7.62MM GATLING MACHINE GUN (1 EACH SIDE)

only a half-load of fuel, and "Heavy Hogs" of Aerial Rocket Artillery (ARA) units also had to reduce their fuel loads significantly.

While able to deliver an extraordinary amount of fire, gunships had their tactical limitations. The weapons were intended for area fire, and had limited effect against point and rapidly moving targets. While 7.62mm, 20mm and 40mm were effective against troops in the open or concealed in moderate vegetation, against light field fortifications and lightly constructed buildings, these calibers had little effect on medium and heavily constructed bunkers and other fortifications; the HE rounds detonated on impact, achieving little penetration.[5] The .50cal achieved moderate results on medium-construction fortifications, but it took a great deal of fire to achieve this owing to inaccuracy, and few of these weapons were mounted on aircraft in any case. The 2.75in rockets could be damaging to bunkers if they achieved hits, but they were notoriously inaccurate. Firing any weapon from a helicopter took a great deal of skill, owing to the constantly changing range, changes in the aircraft's three-dimensional aspects, crosswinds, changes in wind direction and speed at different altitudes, the difficulty of range estimation while moving, and the different angles of attack.

# THE DEVELOPMENT OF AIR MOBILITY

In 1946 the US Army determined that it had a requirement for helicopters for observation, cargo and troop transport, and medical evacuation. While the Army Air Forces had made limited use of crude helicopters from 1944, and had carried out a few rescue missions, the helicopter was basically an unproven technology. The post-war Army was required to procure its aircraft through the Air Force, and that new service was reluctant to acquire helicopters; the USAF believed that they were aerodynamically unsound, and in any case resisted further increases in Army aviation.

[5] See Osprey Fortress 48, *VC and NVA Tunnels and Fortifications*.

During the Korean War only small numbers of helicopters were employed by the Army, mainly for medevac, resupply and liaison; but some farsighted officers could see the potential of the helicopter on the battlefield, even while watching little bubble-nose aircraft struggling to lift two wounded soldiers into the air. It was seen that the rugged terrain and numerical superiority of the enemy could have been partly countered by the large scale use of helicopters. In 1952 the Army ambitiously forecast the need for 12 helicopter battalions, but helicopter development and production limitations prevented this goal being realized.

The event that truly fired the imagination of the Army leadership in regards to airmobility was nothing more than a simple article appearing in *Harper's Magazine*. Entitled "Cavalry, and I Don't Mean Horses!", this was written by MajGen James Gavin, the commander of the 82d AbnDiv in World War II, and appeared in April 1954. Gavin, soon to become Deputy Chief of Staff of the Army, was influential in advancing airmobility, directing the Infantry School at Ft Benning, GA, to develop a tactical doctrine for helicopters. The school's Airborne Department became the Airborne–Army Aviation Dept, with an Airmobility Division to study doctrine, and a helicopter company attached to field-test the concepts under consideration.

In 1956 a provisional "Sky-Cav" platoon was formed by the Aviation School to test armed helicopters, with various combinations of jury-rigged weapons fitted to an assortment of aircraft. The following year this promising unit was redesignated the Aerial Combat Reconnaissance Platoon, and this provided the nucleus for the 7292d Aerial Combat Reconnaissance Company. Continuing research into tactics, armament, and the promise of helicopters then on the drawing board led to the first discussion of an "Armair" division in 1958. Helicopters were still inadequate in performance, and manufacturers were waiting on the Army for guidance as to specifications; they had no idea of what the Army needed – and neither did the Army. This changed in 1959, when the Army Aircraft Development Plan was initiated, recommending that light observation, manned surveillance and tactical transports be developed, both helicopter and fixed-wing.

## The Rogers and Howze Boards

The Army Aircraft Requirements Review Board, or Rogers Board, was established at the beginning of 1960, to match up industry proposals with the Army's needs. One of the most promising proposals was a Bell design called the XH-40 utility helicopter, which would become the UH-1. Originally envisioned as a medevac aircraft, it was soon apparent that it could be employed in numerous other roles. It would replace the H-19, H-21, and H-34 as a light cargo and troop carrier, while the HC-1 Chinook would replace the H-37. A replacement for the H-13 and H-23 observation helicopters was sought, but would be years away. In another area, that same year, the 101st AbnDiv consolidated its aviation resources into the 101st Combat Aviation Battalion (Provisional) – the first such unit.

A major boost was given to the expansion of Army aviation in April 1962, when Secretary of Defense Robert McNamara issued a memorandum stating that the Army's aviation procurement plan was

too conservative, and questioning the mix of aircraft. He was pushing for major changes in force structure and bold new initiatives in the development of tactics. Many of the Army's leadership were too tradition-bound, and McNamara wanted to push them into making major advances in tactical mobility and aerial combat capabilities. The entire aviation structure and procurement was to be looked at anew, and field tests conducted to examine the feasibility of new tactics and doctrine.

To meet this requirement the Army immediately established the Army Tactical Requirements Board, or Howze Board, chaired by LtGen Hamilton Howze, commander of XVIII Airborne Corps. The board's charter gave it a great deal of power to accomplish its many tasks, and its deadlines were demanding. Its remit was to study, test and evaluate all aspects of airmobile unit organization and operations. This was accomplished by exercises and field tests, as well as by the study of past and current aviation operations.

Part of the 82d AbnDiv, Army aviation units, and even Air Force units were allotted to carry out the tests. These field tests compared airmobile and ground-bound forces by pitting them against each other during war games. Over 40 tests were conducted, using 150 Army aircraft; they included live-fire exercises and – presciently? – three week-long exercises against guerrillas.

The Howze Board submitted its report in August 1962; its main recommendation was the establishment of air assault divisions and air cavalry combat brigades with an antitank capability. One of the five alternative programs recommended five air assault divisions, three air cavalry and five air transport brigades, alongside 11 infantry and armored divisions. Aviation assets would be increased in all units to improve their logistics support. The six-year program would require increasing the number of Army aviators from 8,900 to 20,600.

The concept of the air assault division envisaged its having 459 aircraft, but only about one-third of the ground vehicles of an infantry division. One-third of its combat elements could be airlifted in one move by its organic helicopters. It was not simply a question of tactical mobility, however: all aspects of the division's operations would be enhanced by aviation, including reconnaissance, fire support, logistics, command and control, and more. The Howze report survived the variously negative responses of conservative Army officers, a jealous Air Force, and a budget-conscious Congress.

In the meantime, far away in Vietnam, the ARVN was already benefiting from the increasing deployment of US Army and Marine aviation units to become experienced in airmobile operations. In the face of ARVN successes the VC had limited resources to counter the new mobility enjoyed by government troops.

## 11th Air Assault Division (Test)

On February 15, 1963 the cadres for the 11th Air Assault Div and 10th Air Transportation Bde were activated as test units at Ft Benning. These two formations initially possessed only 3,000 personnel and 154 aircraft – the "division" had only one infantry battalion. The test effort would be a challenge; a whole new doctrine had to be developed, for which little guidance or experience existed. At that date it was actually against Army regulations for helicopters to fly in formations. The Air Force remained totally opposed. Bones of contention included the use of the twin-engine, fixed-wing Mohawk surveillance airplane – especially the Army's plan to arm it; armed attack helicopters; and the Caribou twin-engine, fixed-wing transport – all of which the Air Force perceived as incursions into its role.[6]

The 11th Division's commander, MajGen Harry Kinnard, encouraged free thought and listened to any suggestion from subordinates that might enhance the airmobile concept. In spite of shortages of personnel, equipment and aircraft the highly motivated "Skysoldiers" worked long and hard to prove the concept. In September 1963, Exercise "Air Assault I" was conducted as a reinforced battalion war game, which proved very successful. Additional units were raised, including more aviation units. A problem emerged with the Chinook helicopter, however: this proved incapable of meeting its lift and range requirements, and almost scuttled the whole concept, since the division would not be able to accomplish its missions if it did not possess a medium lift logistics helicopter. By now the division had a full brigade; to provide an additional brigade for testing, one was attached from the 2d InfDiv, also at Ft Benning.

There were real concerns about the division's ability to operate at night and in poor weather, its vulnerability to antiaircraft fire, and the maintenance demands of helicopters. Much effort was put into flying under poor conditions, and normal safety requirements were relaxed to allow units to undertake realistic training and push themselves to the maximum extent. Exercise "Air Assault II" was conducted in the Carolinas in October and November 1964; with a hurricane blasting the East Coast and the supporting Air Force aircraft grounded, two of the division's three helicopter battalions found holes in the violent weather, and inserted their troops at their maximum range. The exercise continued regardless of continuing foul weather, and while there were accidents the division proved that the airmobile concept was workable. The exercises had been so successful that "Air Assault III," a division exercise, was cancelled.

---

[6] The Air Force finally won some of these arguments. The Army/Air Force Agreement of January 1, 1967 saw most Army CV-2 Caribous transferred to the Air Force; and the Army gave up on the armed OV-1 Mohawk, retaining it only as a surveillance aircraft. The Army did retain a number of fixed-wing aircraft for utility, liaison, and VIP transport: the U-1 Otter, U-6 Beaver, U-8 Seminole, U-21 Ute, and O-1 Birddog.

May 1962: pushing past the .30cal door gun, ARVN infantry quickly off-load from a US Army H-21B (later redesignated CH-21B) during early airmobile operations against the Viet Cong. There was no troop door on the right side, and the VC knew which side the troops would emerge. The original caption does not identify the US unit; it does stress that US personnel were advisors, not in combat status, and were instructed to fire only if fired upon. Note the conspicuous full-color markings still applied to aircraft at this early stage of American involvement in the war. (US Army, courtesy Simon Dunstan)

### 1st Cavalry Division (Airmobile)

The partially formed 11th Air Assault Div's capabilities were felt to be so well suited for a response to the worsening situation in Vietnam that a decision was taken to expand it to a full division, and to deploy it to Southeast Asia as soon as possible. On June 15, 1965 it was redesignated the 1st Cavalry Div (Airmobile), using the assets of the 11th Air Assault and 2d Infantry Divs, 10th Air Transportation Bde, and additional helicopter units drawn from throughout the Army.

At the time the 1st CavDiv was serving in Korea. Its colors were swapped with those of the 2d InfDiv, as it was thought that the cavalry designation would effectively describe the division capabilities as "air cavalry."[7] The division was to be fully manned and equipped by the end of July 1965; a major effort was made to achieve this, with every unit and depot fair game for requisition. At the time the division had only 9,500 of its required 15,900 personnel, and half of the assigned troops were due for discharge or otherwise ineligible for overseas deployment, among them hundreds of experienced aircrewmen and maintenance personnel. Additional aircrew were arriving who had not yet flown the division's new helicopters.

A 1,000-man advance party was airlifted to Vietnam in August 1965 to prepare a base of operations near the An Khe Special Forces camp in the Central Highlands. At the end of July the division began its sea movement aboard six troop transports, 14 cargo ships, and an amphibious assault ship. The division arrived in September, and in late October it commenced offensive airmobile operations in the enemy-controlled Ia Drang Valley to interdict NVA units entering Vietnam from Cambodia. (These operations are studied in the book *We Were Soldiers Once…and Young* – see below, "Further Reading".) An entirely new concept of warfare was introduced to the world.

# AIRMOBILE UNITS IN VIETNAM

The 1st Cavalry Div (Airmobile) could be moved by air both tactically and strategically. Other divisions were airmobile to some degree, but required considerable non-divisional helicopter and Air Force airlift support; some of their equipment would have to be left behind, especially tanks and heavy engineer equipment, and a massive number of airlift sorties were necessary. The much more lightly equipped airmobile division "weighed" only about one-third as much as an infantry division, and was also routinely trained to conduct such movements. Everything could be moved strategically by C-130 transports, with the exception of CH-47 Chinooks, which required C-133 transports. For deployment by ship,

---

[7] It is rumored that the 1st CavDiv once lost its colors in an unspecified war, and that its colors were not to be returned to the United States. This is a myth.

which was the more common means of strategic deployment, the airmobile division required much less shipping space than a standard division.

Once in the theater of operations the airmobile division possessed a phenomenal degree of tactical mobility. If moving from one part of Vietnam to another, the helicopters made multiple lifts depending on the distance. Much of the personnel and equipment would be moved by intra-theater transports – CV-2s, C-123s and C-130s. Sometimes heavy equipment was convoyed to the new area of operations. This tactical mobility provided the division with a great deal of flexibility, and distinctive capabilities in all combat environments:

Before the colors of the 214th Aviation Battalion (Combat), the company commanders salute and their guidons (in white on ultramarine blue) are dipped – those of the 114th, 135th, 175th, 199th and 335th Aviation Companies. All were assault helicopter companies with Hueys except the 199th, which was a reconnaissance airplane company with Mohawks. In 1969 the battalion was located at Vinh Long in the Mekong Delta. (Leroy "Red" Wilson)

It could move rapidly and directly to key objective areas over any terrain, and deliver troops fresh and ready for immediate combat.

It could maintain very rapid and high intensity operations, and respond swiftly to changes in the tactical situation.

It could disengage at one point, and move rapidly in any direction to fight at another point a considerable distance away.

It could engage the enemy by exploiting his vertical flanks for quick in-and-out actions.

It could rapidly exploit opportunities presented by the enemy, or reinforce advantages achieved by other friendly forces.

It could traverse difficult terrain, and obstacles such as rivers, mountains, swamps, and areas of destruction or contamination that would halt or delay ground forces.

It could provide itself with extensive aerial fire support.

It could support itself logistically using organic aircraft.

The airmobile division was envisioned as being capable of fighting in either a chemical, biological and nuclear war; a conventional war, conducting contingency operations in Third World counties; or combating an insurgency. It proved ideal for use in Vietnam, its organic assets allowing it to operate in larger areas of operation over difficult terrain. Its flexibility, and ability to introduce large forces into remote areas quickly, kept the enemy off balance: the air cavalrymen could arrive at any time, from any direction, with little or no warning. It was also able at short notice to dispatch aerial fire support, introduce reinforcements, resupply engaged forces, evacuate casualties, and extract forces from unfavorable positions. Its organic aerial reconnaissance and target acquisition capabilities were extensive.

### From Airborne to Airmobile

The 101st AbnDiv's 1st Bde deployed to Vietnam in July 1965, and the remainder of the division arrived in November 1967. The 1st Bde was followed by the 173d Abn Bde (Separate). The Army was unable to produce enough paratroopers for all the airborne units worldwide,

Operation "Todd Forest," 1969: the "screaming eagle" (or as some called it, "puking buzzard" or "vomiting vulture") insignia of 101st AbnDiv is clearly visible on this Dust-Off chopper of 326th Medical Bn, picking up walking wounded from 1st Bn, 506th Inf near Hue. (US Army, courtesy Simon Dunstan)

but large airborne units were not needed in Vietnam. The 101st was converted to airmobile, a process that began in July 1969, with the last units taken off jump status the following month. Existing units' tables of organization were changed, and additional aviation units assigned, to provide the same organization as the 1st CavDiv.

The Americal Division (aka 23d InfDiv) was organized in Vietnam from existing light infantry brigades and other units in September 1967. In February 1969 it was reorganized as other infantry divisions, but an aviation group of three battalions was assigned. While not under the airmobile division table of organization, it did partly possess such capabilities.

All infantry units in Vietnam, whether standard, light, airborne, airmobile, or even mechanized, became equally proficient in the conduct of airmobile operations. Unneeded heavy weapons and equipment were left behind, and unit leaders and troops easily learned the necessary procedures and skills.

## The aviators

The heart of aviation units was the Army aviators – the pilots. These were either commissioned officers, or they underwent the Warrant Officer Aviator Program prior to entering 32 weeks of flight training. This was followed by various lengths of transition training on their primary helicopter. The need for pilots in Vietnam was so great that most new aviators were deployed directly without assignment to a Stateside aviation unit to gain experience. To make up for this lack of operational experience, once arrived in Vietnam they would be given a check-ride to verify their knowledge and skills. Regardless of rank, they would be

A Huey door gunner – note M60D spade grips at top left – wearing the APH-4 aviator's helmet with M33A microphone; the APH-5 was similar. They were issued in olive drab, but colored bands and unit decals were sometimes applied. Just visible on his shoulder is the subdued patch of the 1st Avn Bde, worn by most non-divisional aviation units. (Leroy "Red" Wilson)

assigned a co-pilot's seat and fly 25 hours of administrative missions before being given a duty assignment.

The demand for pilots was insatiable. With more and more units flowing into Vietnam, and helicopter production reaching an all-time high, they could not be trained fast enough. The Army refused to lower standards, and every rated aviator, from major on down, was assigned a cockpit seat. Aviators, unlike other personnel, were being sent back to Vietnam for subsequent tours in under two years. The 2,000 Army Reserve aviators were requested to consider active duty, but only 60 accepted. The numbers of aviators in other theaters were cut to the bone – only 250 were left in Europe, and 34 in Korea.

The instrument console of a UH-1B or -C Huey. The pilots' armored seats and their side panels can be seen; a lever allowed the seat to be tipped backwards so that a wounded pilot could be extracted. In all, more than 40,000 helicopter pilots from all services served in Vietnam; of those, 2,197 were killed by all causes, along with 2,724 non-pilot crewmen. (Leroy "Red" Wilson)

It was projected that in 1966 the Army would need 14,300 aviators, but despite all these expedients only 9,700 would be available, including new graduates – of which only 120 per month were being produced in that year. In 1967 the requirement would be 21,500, with only 12,800 available. The Aviation School did manage to increase monthly output to 200 graduates, but over twice that number were needed. To alleviate this shortage the flight schools at Ft Rucker and Ft Wolters were expanded, and at the same time a new Army Flight Training Center was opened at Ft Stewart, GA. The supply of aviators improved, but shortages persisted throughout the war.

The **Marine Corps** had its own problems obtaining sufficient helicopter pilots, who were obtained through the Platoon Leader Class (Aviation), an ROTC-like program, the Aviation Officer Candidate Course, and the Marine Corps Aviation Cadet program. All Marine pilots were commissioned officers; there were no warrant officer pilots, and this limited the number of qualified personnel. Another problem was that the Marines had their own air arm, with three categories of pilots: jet, propeller-driven, and helicopter. Near the end of basic flight training allocations were forecast for the number of pilots needed in each category. The top rated group was allowed to select the type they desired, with most choosing jets; the second group was assigned to prop-driven fixed-wing aircraft, and the lowest group to helicopters. This practice made helicopter pilots "second-class citizens" within Marine Aviation.

In 1962 a limited warrant officer pilot program was initiated, but this required reserve commissioned officers and separated officers returning to the service to give up their commissions in order to fly; few applied. The situation was critical in 1962; because of their perceived low status some helicopter pilots were leaving the Marines, with some even going to the Army. Marine helicopters required 40 percent of the Corps' pilots, but only 29 percent were assigned to such duty. Some 500 jet and prop pilots were notified that they would be re-trained as helicopter pilots and serve a tour as such. A few actually resigned, but most did their duty – and found that flying helicopters was not as easy as they had thought. After that, 20 fixed-wing pilots were selected for helicopter

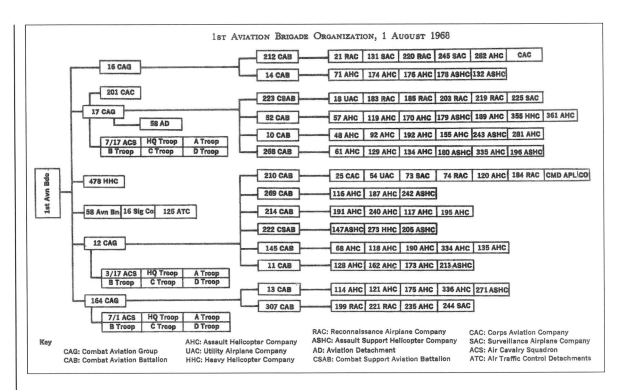

1ST AVIATION BRIGADE ORGANIZATION, 1 AUGUST 1968

Key
CAG: Combat Aviation Group
CAB: Combat Aviation Battalion
AHC: Assault Helicopter Company
UAC: Utility Airplane Company
HHC: Heavy Helicopter Company
RAC: Reconnaissance Airplane Company
ASHC: Assault Support Helicopter Company
AD: Aviation Detachment
CSAB: Combat Support Aviation Battalion
CAC: Corps Aviation Company
SAC: Surveillance Airplane Company
ACS: Air Cavalry Squadron
ATC: Air Traffic Control Detachments

training each month; apart from providing sufficient pilots, the goal was to eliminate the "second-class syndrome." Marine helicopter training was conducted with the Navy at Naval Air Station Pensacola, FL; later, some Marines received training from the Army.

### The airmobile division

Airmobile units fell into two categories. The airmobile division possessed the full range of combined arms and supporting units as other divisions, and included significantly larger organic aviation assets. Other divisions possessed an organic aviation battalion. There were also many non-divisional aviation units, from company to brigade in size.

Organizationally the airmobile division was similar to a standard infantry division. The airmobile division was assigned 15,786 troops, but this figure rose considerably with attachments. It had fewer and often lighter vehicles and trailers. Heavy equipment items, especially engineer and signal, were replaced with lighter items, and in some categories lighter weapons were provided. Its total of some 1,600 vehicles was about half that of an infantry division; but it was assigned a vastly larger organic aviation force – 434 helicopters (before reinforcement by other aviation units), in place of the 100 of an infantry division. Airmobile infantry battalions were much more lightly equipped and manned than their standard counterparts. When it arrived in Vietnam, the 1st CavDiv (Airmobile) had only eight infantry battalions, three of which were also airborne-qualified; it later received a ninth battalion.[8] The division's battalions carried the lineages of former cavalry units, and were designated, for instance, 1st Battalion (Airmobile), 7th Cavalry. The 101st AbnDiv (Airmobile) had ten battalions. The battalions could be

---

[8] 1st Bde HHC, an artillery battalion, and an engineer company were also Airborne. All these units lost this distinction in November 1966, owing to the rotation of personnel and the Army's inability to train enough paratroopers.

## Table of Organization, Airmobile Division

| Element | Helicopters | Element | Helicopters |
|---|---|---|---|
| Division HQ & HQ Company | | Transportation Aircraft Maintenance | |
| Brigade HQ & HQ Co (x3) | 2x UH-1B, 8x OH-13 | & Supply Bn | 8x UH-1D, 8x OH-13 |
| Infantry Battalion (Airmobile) | | Medical Bn | 12x UH-1D |
| (x8-10) | | Administrative Co | |
| *Division Artillery* | | Air Cavalry Squadron | 38x UH-1B, 20x UH-1D, |
| HQ & HQ Battery | | | 30x OH-13 |
| Artillery Bn (105mm howitzer) (x3) | | Engineer Combat Bn | |
| Artillery Bn (155mm howitzer) | | Signal Bn | |
| Artillery Bn (Aerial Rocket) | 43x UH-1B | Military Police Co | |
| Artillery Bty (Aviation) | 12x OH-13 | | |
| *Aviation Group* | | *Typical attachments:* | |
| HQ & HQ Co | | Artillery Bn (105mm howitzer) | |
| Aviation Bn (Assault Helicopter) (x2) | 60x UH-1D, 12x UH-1B | Artillery Bn (155mm howitzer) | |
| | 3x OH-13 | Aviation Co (Heavy Helicopter) | 4–5x CH-54 |
| Aviation Bn (Assault Support | | Infantry LRRP/Ranger Co | |
| Helicopter) | 28x CH-47, 3x OH-13 | Army Security Agency Co | |
| Aviation Co (General Support) | 16x UH-1B/D, 10x OH-13, | Military Intelligence Co/Detachment | |
| | 6x OV-1 | Chemical Det/Platoon | |
| *Division Support Command* | | Public Information Det | |
| HQ & HQ Co & Band | | Infantry Det (Ground Surveillance Radar) | |
| Ordnance Maintenance Bn | | Infantry Platoon (Scout Dog) | |
| Quartermaster Supply & Service Bn | | Infantry Platoon (Combat Tracker) | |

attached to the three brigades as necessary, typically three to each. An additional 105mm and a 155mm artillery battalion were added to the two divisions, which otherwise differed in their attachments.

The infantry battalions each comprised a headquarters and head-quarter company (communications, support, maintenance platoons; battalion HQ section); three rifle companies (weapons platoon and three rifle platoons); and combat support company (scout, mortar, antitank platoons) – in 1968 this became a fourth rifle company, to provide a company to secure a firebase and still field three companies.

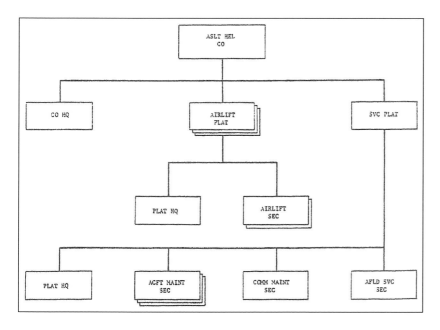

Organization of an assault helicopter company – the troop-lifting components of the aviation battalion (assault helicopter).

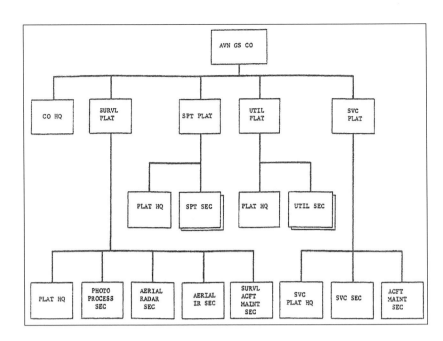

Organization of an aviation company (general support) – a separate asset of the divisional aviation group.

The field artillery battalions each had a headquarters battery and three howitzer batteries with six tubes each. A fourth battery was added to 105mm battalions in 1968; prior to that, some battalions formed a fourth provisional battery by taking two howitzers each from two of their batteries. Initially the World War II-era 105mm M101A1 howitzer was used, but in March 1966 the lighter weight M102 began to replace it in Army battalions (though not in the Marines). While it still had to be lifted by a CH-47, the M102's lighter weight allowed more gun crew and ammunition to be carried inside the chopper.

Besides the three-battalion aviation group, other divisional units possessed organic helicopters. The three brigade headquarters each had an aviation section of eight choppers for C&C and liaison. Division artillery had a large ARA battalion, plus a company-size battery with LOHs for artillery spotting. The medical battalion had its own medevac choppers; and even the aviation maintenance battalion had 16 helicopters for flying in maintenance contact teams and spare parts.

The numbers and types of helicopters are listed in the table of organization on page 27. In practice the number varied, and might be higher. The OH-13 began to be replaced by the OH-6A in 1968; from mid-1967, AH-1G Cobras began to replace the UH-1B/C gunships; and the UH-1D was gradually replaced by the UH-1H beginning in 1967.

**Pathfinders**
The Pathfinders originated during World War II as specially trained volunteer paratroopers who would jump into enemy territory just prior to parachute and glider assaults, to locate and mark drop and landing zones by means of radio beacons, lights, smoke and panels. They recorded variable success in these missions. In the mid-1950s the Army almost lost this capability due to inter-service agreements by which the Air Force's new Combat Control Teams would take over the mission of marking and operating drop zones when troops were dropped by Air Force transports. However, it was realized that Pathfinders were still

needed by the Army to mark and operate DZs for paratroopers dropped from helicopters, and to establish and operate LZs and airstrips for Army helicopters and fixed-wing aircraft.

Pathfinders were essentially tactical air controllers for use in the combat zone. Officially their primary mission was to provide navigational assistance and control of Army aircraft in areas of operations designated by supported unit commanders:

to enter areas of operations by foot, water, ground vehicles, aircraft or parachute;

to reconnoiter and select landing and drop zones;

to furnish air-to-ground communications to aircraft;

to provide advice to aviators concerning artillery and mortar fires through coordination with co-located fire support units;

to provide advice and limited physical assistance for preparing and positioning troops, equipment and supplies for air movement;

to provide limited local weather observations affecting airmobile/airborne operations;

to assist in rigging and attaching vehicle/cargo sling loads; and

to operate, by mutual agreement with the Air Force, drop and landing zones and airfields in the absence of Air Force Combat Control Teams.

Infantry/airborne division and non-divisional aviation battalions had a Pathfinder section comprising two lieutenants and 13 enlisted men, who operated in two to four teams as required. The airmobile division's aviation group had a Pathfinder detachment of four such sections. The 1st CavDiv formed the 11th Pathfinder Co (Provisional) prior to its deployment to Vietnam, to serve under the 11th Aviation Group. Pathfinders were required to be infantrymen (eight weeks' Basic Combat Training, eight weeks' Light Weapons Infantryman Advanced Individual Training); to be parachute-qualified (three weeks); and to attend the Pathfinder School (three weeks) at Ft Benning. Because of their scarcity and the unceasing demand for infantrymen, few aviation units actually possessed Pathfinder units. One reason for this was that once infantry and aviation units had become routinely acquainted with airmobile operations, there was little need for the specialized skills of Pathfinders. Many units possessing Pathfinders when they deployed to Vietnam let the units dwindle away as Pathfinders rotated home. Some

Plei Me, November 1965: a wounded trooper from Co C, 2d Bn, 8th Cavalry is rushed to a UH-1D Dust-Off bird of the Air Ambulance Platoon, 15th Medical Battalion. Even though the enemy chose not to respect the Geneva Cross, it was still marked on helicopters; it remained important for US troops to be able to recognize medevac ships quickly. (US Army, courtesy Simon Dunstan)

Generically known as the "attack helicopter company," this element was formally designated an aviation company (aerial weapons) (AW) and in some instances as an aviation company (escort).

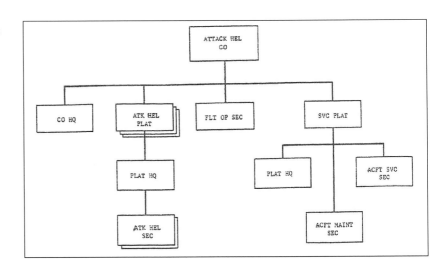

aviation units did retain Pathfinders, or later established a Pathfinder unit if a new commander felt the need. These often consisted of one officer and a few Pathfinder-qualified NCOs, the rest of the unqualified personnel learning their skills on the job.

Since it was neither practical nor necessary to insert Pathfinders on LZs in hostile territory, they were relegated to serving as air controllers at firebases with high air traffic, and assisted in the marshaling of units and launching operations. They sometimes went in with the first lifts to provide air traffic control if the LZ was to remain in use to support a ground operation, and would continue to operate as an LZ was closed down and the units departed. They earned their motto, "First in, last out."

**Army aviation units**

The airmobile division's two *assault helicopter battalions* each had a headquarters company, an aerial weapons company (three platoons), and three *assault helicopter companies* (two platoons) with Hueys. Separate assault helicopter companies had two platoons of slicks and one of gunships. The *assault support helicopter battalion* had a headquarters company and three assault support helicopter companies (two platoons) with Chinooks.

*Aviation battalion headquarter companies* had a company headquarters and battalion headquarters, communications, medical, and maintenance and supply sections. Non-divisional aviation battalion headquarters were similarly organized, but included small S1 (personnel), S2/S3 (intelligence, operations), and S4 (supply) sections plus an air traffic control platoon. An *aviation company*, regardless of type, in addition to its two to four helicopter platoons, had a flight operations section, to establish and operate the company heliport and assist the headquarters with operational control. It also had a service platoon with aircraft maintenance and aircraft service sections; the platoon provided unit-level maintenance and servicing of the company's aircraft, vehicles, weapons and avionics.

Just as in the armored cavalry, air cavalry squadrons and troops were battalion- and company-size units respectively. Aviation battalions/squadrons were commanded by lieutenant-colonels, companies/batteries/troops by majors, and platoons by captains. Helicopter platoons were subdivided into two sections commanded by lieutenants. The number of aircraft assigned to the platoon depended on the type. All of these officers were rated aviators and flew their own helicopters; all other helicopters were piloted by warrant officers. Non-aviation companies and platoons were commanded by captains and lieutenants respectively.

The infantry and airborne divisions' *combat aviation battalion* was a small unit providing minimal support to its parent division. Divisions would additionally be supported by units of the aviation group responsible for their area. The combat aviation battalion had a headquarters company, an assault helicopter company (three platoons), and a general support aviation company. The headquarters company was organized like those of the airmobile division's aviation battalions, but had the addition of an air traffic control platoon, airspace control team, and (in the airborne division only) a Pathfinder section. In Vietnam an air cavalry troop was attached to the divisional armored cavalry squadron; other aviation companies might be temporarily attached to the divisional aviation battalion.

The airmobile division possessed a battalion-size *air cavalry squadron* with a headquarters troop, a ground cavalry troop, and three air cavalry troops. Air cavalry troops were organized into three unique platoons: an aero weapons platoon with 11 gunships ("Guns" or "Reds"), an aero scout platoon with 10 Loachs ("Scouts" or "Whites"), and an aero rifle platoon ("Blues") with four rifle squads carried by a lift section of five Hueys. There were two divisional (1–9 and 2–17 Cav) and three non-divisional air cav squadrons (7–1, 3–17 and 7–17 Cavalry) in Vietnam.

Airmobile divisions had an *aviation general support company* like the infantry divisions, but with the addition of 6x twin-engine OV-1B/C Mohawk surveillance aircraft fitted with side-looking radar or infrared cameras. The division artillery was assigned an *aerial rocket artillery battalion* with three batteries of 12x rocket-only armed Hueys, and an *aviation artillery battery* equipped with 12x Loachs for artillery spotting. A *heavy helicopter company* with 4–5x "Flying Cranes" was attached to the aviation group. The brigade headquarters had an aviation platoon with 2x Hueys and 8x Loachs. *Aerial weapons companies* were pure gunship units, with two platoons. Separate brigades often had an air assault company attached.

*Air ambulance companies* (24x Hueys in four platoons) and detachments (6x UH-1H) provided critical medical evacuation, and were assigned specific areas or units to support. Unarmed medevac Hueys were fitted with six litters (stretchers) and a rescue hoist, invaluable for extracting casualties where no LZ was available. A medical aidman was part of the crew.

Most aviation units were non-divisional assets. A wide variety of separate aviation companies, batteries, and air cavalry troops were deployed to Vietnam – more than 140 of all types. For control purposes they were attached to *combat* or *combat support aviation battalions*, of which 16 served in Vietnam. Companies were frequently transferred between battalions; anything from three to six companies of different types might be attached at a given time. *Combat aviation groups*, of which seven served in Vietnam (11th 12th, 16th, 17th, 160th, 164th, 165th), controlled aviation units within specific areas to support US, ARVN, and Free World forces in their area. Two to six aviation battalions and several separate companies might be attached to a group, together with – usually – an air cavalry squadron.

## Types of Army Aviation Companies

| Company/Troop/Battery | Abbreviation | Aircraft |
|---|---|---|
| Aviation (Airmobile) (Light)/ Assault Helicopter | AML/AHC | 23x UH-1D/H, 8x UH-1C |
| Aerial Weapons | AWC | 12x UH-1C |
| Medium Helicopter/ Assault Support Helicopter | MH/ASHC | 16x CH-47, 2x OH-6 |
| Heavy Helicopter | HH | 4–5x CH-54A/B |
| General Support Aviation | GS | 16x UH-1B/D, 10x OH-6, 6x OV-1B/C |
| Air Ambulance | Air Ambul Co | 24x UH-1D/H |
| Air Cavalry Troop | Air Cav Trp | 11x AH-1, 10x OH-6, 8x UH-1 |
| Aerial Rocket Artillery Battery | ARA Bty | 12x UH-1C |
| Artillery Battery (Aviation) | Arty Bty (Avn) | 12x OH-6 |

*Note:* Aviation companies (airmobile) (light), and medium helicopter companies, were redesignated "assault helicopter" and "assault support helicopter" companies, respectively, by July 1966. From 1967 to 1971, AH-1Gs replaced UH-1C gunships.

To control the scores of aviation units in Vietnam, the 1st Aviation Bde was activated in-country on May 25, 1966 at Tan Son Nhut Air Base in Saigon. At its peak it controlled over 4,200 aircraft, of which over 600 were fixed-wing, and some 24,000 personnel. While commanded by a brigadier general, it was a division-level command operating the length and breadth of the country. One of its main goals was to standardize operating procedures, tactics, maintenance and aviation supplies allocation. It was not entirely successful in this endeavor, owing to the many diversified units and methods of operation dictated by the widely varied terrain, climatic and tactical situations. The command were relocated to Long Binh outside of Saigon in December 1967, and in December 1972 back to Tan Son Nhut, where it remained until it departed Vietnam the following March.

### Marine aviation units

In Vietnam all Marine Aviation assets – whether jet fighters, transports, utility aircraft or helicopters – were under the 1st Marine Aircraft Wing (MAW). 1st MAW was originally based at Iwakuni, Japan, with elements on Okinawa. In 1962 it had begun deploying units to Vietnam with Marine Task Force "Shufly" and later with Marine Unit, Vietnam (1964).

Major deployments began in March 1965; 1st MAW established an advanced command post in Da Nang in May, and its main headquarters deployed there in June. 1st MAW maintained a rear echelon at Iwakuni until April 1966, when it became responsible only for units in Vietnam. Marine air units in the Western Pacific rotated fixed-wing squadrons between Japan and Vietnam, and helicopter squadrons between Okinawa, afloat with the 7th Fleet Special Landing Force, and Vietnam. All types of squadrons conducted 13-month rotations from the States to the Western Pacific and consequently rotated into Vietnam.

A Marine CH-46A approaches an amphibious assault transport (LPH). One or two of these ships operated off the coast of Vietnam, carrying a "special landing force" – a reinforced battalion landing team, that could be landed by landing craft, amphibious tractor or helicopter to reinforce forces ashore. Marine helicopters were painted in forest green with white markings.

*(continued on page 41)*

**AIRCRAFT RECOVERY, AND EARLY HELICOPTERS**

1: CH-37B Mojave

2: CH-21C Shawnee

A

**TROOP LIFT**
**1: UH-1D "slick"**
**2: UH-1C "hog"**

B

**AERIAL FIRE SUPPORT**
1: AH-1G Hueycobra
2: OH-6A Cayuse

**CONDUCT OF AN AIRMOBILE ASSAULT (1)**
See text commentary for details

D

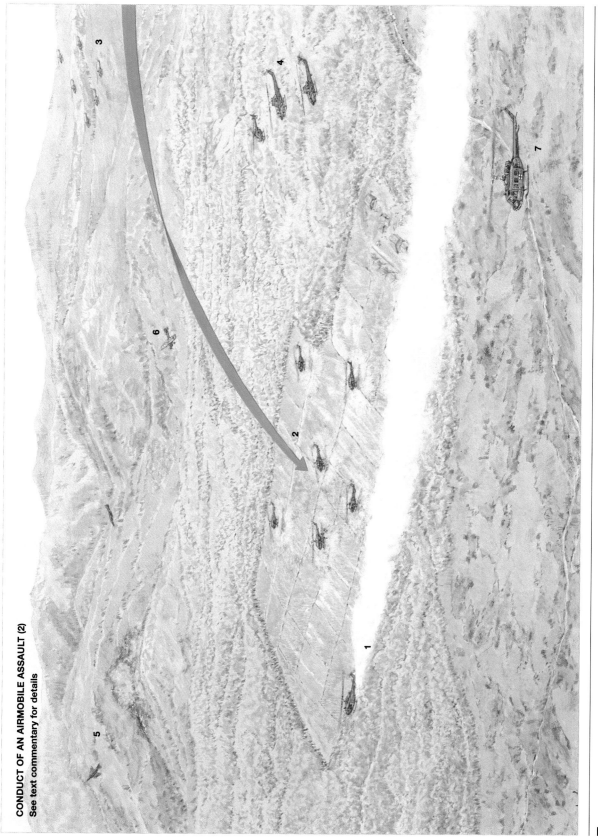

E

**ARTILLERY RAID**
1: CH-47A Chinook
2: M102 105mm howitzer

F

**MARINE AIR ASSAULT**
1: CH-53A Sea Stallion
2: CH-46D Sea Knight
3: M274 Mechanical Mule

**G**

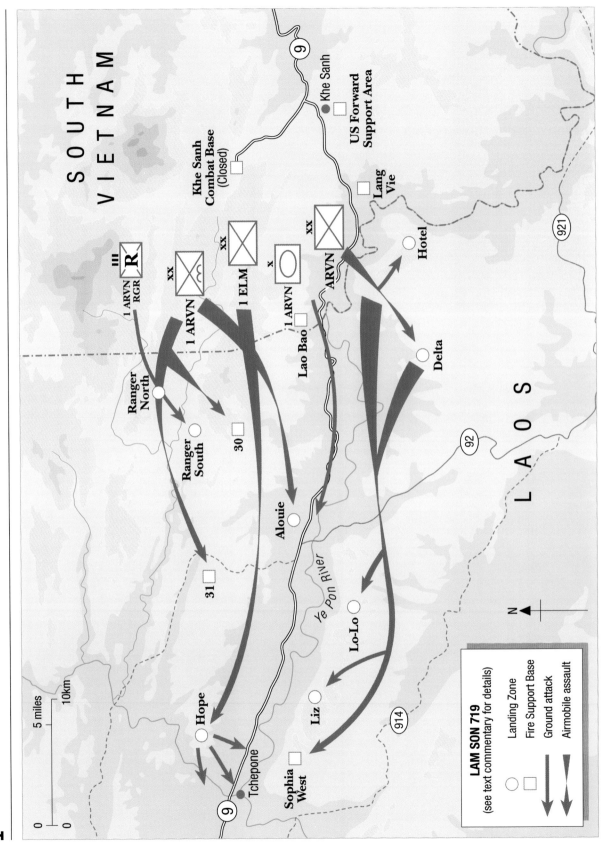

H

SOUTH VIETNAM

LAOS

Khe Sanh Combat Base (Closed)

Khe Sanh

US Forward Support Area

Lang Vie

Hotel

Delta

III R
1 ARVN RGR

xx
1 ARVN

xx
1 ELM

x
1 ARVN

xx
ARVN

Lao Bao

Ranger North

Ranger South

30

31

Alouie

Ye Pon River

Lo-Lo

Liz

Hope

Tchepone

Sophia West

9

9

921

92

914

N

5 miles

10km

0

0

**LAM SON 719**
(see text commentary for details)

Landing Zone

Fire Support Base

Ground attack

Airmobile assault

August 1965: a flight of UH-34D "Huss" choppers of HMM-161, 1st MAW, carry Marines low across a high, thickly forested ridge before making a beeline for an LZ beyond, to limit enemy reaction time. This is a graphic image of one of the main advantages of airmobility. (US Marine Corps, courtesy Simon Dunstan)

The 1st MAW had three fixed-wing aircraft groups and two of helicopters, Marine Aircraft Groups (MAG) -16 and -36, both of which arrived in 1965. A Provisional MAG-39 was formed in March 1968 and closed out at the end of 1969. Three main Marine helicopter bases were established in I CTZ at Phu Bai, Marble Mountain outside Da Nang, and Ky Ha outside Chu Lai. MAG-36 departed in November 1969 with some of its squadrons, the remaining squadrons being reassigned to MAG-16. MAGs were commanded by colonels.

Marine helicopter squadrons were commanded by lieutenant colonels. Internal organization varied depending on the number and type of aircraft; there were generally three or more divisions, of six to eight helicopters each, divided into sections of two to four aircraft. Marine squadrons were identified by three-letter codes, the first being "H" for helicopter or "V" for fixed-wing; the second letter was "M" for Marine (Navy aviation units lack a service identifier), and the third the type of unit: "M" = medium, "H" = heavy, "L" = light, and "O" = observation. Although designated as fixed-wing, VMO observation squadrons also possessed helicopters.

Medium helicopter squadrons (HMM) were equipped with 24x UH-34s or, from 1967/68, 21x CH-46s, and were employed for cargo and troop lift. Heavy helicopter squadrons (HMH) had 18x CH-53s; they moved artillery, vehicles and heavy cargo, carried out aircraft recovery, and also delivered troops in secure areas. Four HMHs and 13 HMMs served in Vietnam at one time or another, some serving multiple tours.

The assignment of aircraft to observation (VMO) and light helicopter (HML) squadrons changed. Initially VMOs had O-1B (OE-1 Navy designation) Birddog spotter airplanes and UH-1E helicopters, some of the latter being armed. In 1967 VMOs began changing to a mix of 18x OV-10A Bronco twin-engine observation/attack aircraft and 24x UH-1Es. In a one-year period in 1966–67 it was found that 10,745 sorties by UH-1Es were administrative, liaison, air traffic control, medevac, C&C, search-and-rescue and reconnaissance; another 19,697 missions were as attack helicopters and armed escort. Clearly a delineation had to be made. Half of the UH-1Es were reassigned to two new HMLs with 25x armed UH-1Es, one of these squadrons being converted from a VMO; the two remaining VMOs now had 18x OV-10s and 12x UH-1Es, or all OV-10s. In early 1969 the HMLs began receiving AH-1G Cobras.

The Marines were not comfortable with the idea of helicopter gunships, and preferred jet fighter-bombers; but conditions in Vietnam demanded gunship support, and jets were not always ideal for the tactical situation. This was particularly so when the aerial fire support had to loiter in the area, or escort troop lift helicopters – tasks which could not be accomplished by jets.

# AVIATION MISSIONS

Aviation units could perform a wide variety of tasks in both defensive and offensive operations. Not all of these missions were necessary in Vietnam, and others were seldom undertaken:
adjustment of fire;
aerial photography;
aeromedical evacuation;
aircraft recovery;
airlift of materiel (resupply);
airlift of personnel (anyone from assault troops to VIPs);
battlefield illumination;
chemical agent delivery (including smoke screens and defoliants);
close air support (direct aerial fires);
command and control;
courier flights;
counterbattery;
electronic countermeasures;
electronic warfare support measures;
message drop and pick-up;
psychological operations support (leaflets and loudspeakers);
radiological survey;
radio retransmission;
reconnaissance and surveillance;
search and rescue;
topographic survey;
wire-laying; and
evacuation of prisoners and captured weapons, supplies, and materials.

As with any capability, airmobility faced limitations. Vulnerability to enemy air defenses, including enemy aircraft, was of course the primary concern. Aircraft on the ground and their support facilities (parking, refueling, maintenance areas) were vulnerable to enemy ground action; in Vietnam this took the form of rocket, mortar, and sapper (reconnaissance-commando) attacks. Aviation also required a high volume of logistics support owing to high consumption rates of fuel, oils, lubricants, ammunition and replacement parts. Relatively high

The USNS *Corpus Christi Bay* (T-ARVH-1) was a 527ft long aircraft repair ship, converted from a seaplane tender in 1966 to handle helicopters, and docked at Vung Tau and Cam Ranh Bay as a floating rebuild facility between 1966 and 1972. Two Hueys or one Chinook could land on the aft platform for repair; the forward platform took Hueys for liaison and parts delivery. The ship was manned by the 360-strong 1st Transportation Bn (Aircraft Maintenance Depot, Seaborne), and a 130-man civilian contract crew.

maintenance requirements resulted in frequent and lengthy maintenance and repairs; up to one-fifth of a unit's aircraft could be "down" at any one time, although units attempted to maintain at least 75 percent availability.

## Maintenance

Not enough attention has been paid to the efforts of maintenance personnel, which included helicopter mechanics, armament and avionics specialists and crew chiefs at all echelons. The crew chiefs, usually specialist 5s (equivalent to sergeants), were trained mechanics who oversaw the maintenance of their aircraft. Pilots might switch off and walk away from the aircraft, but the crew chief stayed with *his* bird. After flying as a door gunner, and supervising the loading and unloading of passengers, he often stayed up most of the night maintaining, repairing, and performing required inspections on his aircraft, along with other maintenance personnel. Night test flights were prohibited elsewhere, but were necessary in Vietnam. Many crew chiefs were unofficially trained in the rudiments of flying a helicopter, and there were instances of them saving the aircraft when the pilots became casualties; this was especially true in LOHs, which carried only a single pilot.

The environment in Vietnam had an adverse effect on helicopters. They flew excessive hours, and the maintenance schedules were not always achievable on a timely basis. Average flight time was programmed at 70 hours a month, but it was not uncommon for helicopters to log 100–150 hours. The dust and heat took its toll on engines and rotor blades. Complete engine and transmission replacement was much more frequent than under normal conditions; and blades expected to last 1,000 hours were wearing out in 200 because of heavy loads, debris strikes, and sand erosion.

Besides organic aviation maintenance units, the General Support Group (Aircraft Maintenance and Support) (Provisional) was established at Tan Son Nhut Airbase in 1965 as the primary aircraft maintenance facility and depot. It was redesignated the 34th General Support Group (Aviation Support) the following year. Owing to shortages of maintenance personnel much of the Group's work was done by contracted civilians. Seven transportation aircraft maintenance battalions served in Vietnam.

July 1967: this Army UH-1H "slick" from 9th Avn Bn, 9th InfDiv lands on the 16ft square platform added above the troop compartment of a Navy "Tango boat" – Armored Troop Carrier – of River Assault Flotilla One, operating in the Mekong Delta. Initial limited experiments with the "world's smallest aircraft carrier" were followed by a general modification of these boats to ATC (Helicopter) standard. (US Navy, courtesy Simon Dunstan)

## Climate and weather

The effects of adverse climate and weather hampered flight operations. In Vietnam high heat and humidity, and in the north high altitudes, all limited lift capacity. Low cloud and fog posed problems, especially in the mountainous north, where they severely limited flying conditions. The battle for Khe Sanh, which relied entirely on air support for resupply and fire support, was seriously affected by local conditions. During the monsoon season, heavy rains often fell daily at the same time, the exact times changing slightly every few weeks but remaining regular. This predictability allowed flight operations to be planned around the rainy periods. High winds were seldom encountered in Vietnam, but could affect operations. For the UH-1 a maximum wind speed for start-up was 30 knots, or a 15-knot gust spread; a Huey could hover in a maximum 30-knot crosswind or downwind. Night operations were usually limited to small-scale emergency missions, and night vision devices of the period were inadequate. A constant factor was restricted load carrying capabilities, additionally affected by the necessary long ranges.

## Airmobile missions

Along with the tasks listed above, airmobile forces could perform a wide variety of missions; again, not all were applicable to Vietnam, but most were:
delivery of ground forces into an area of operations;
seizure and retention of key terrain;
envelopment and over-obstacle operations;
raids;
counter-airborne, counter-airmobile, and counter-guerrilla operations;
exploitation of nuclear and special weapons and conventional bomber strikes;
reconnaissance and security missions to block or screen enemy avenues of approach, e.g. covering force, flank guard, and rear area security;
feints and demonstrations;
economy-of-force missions;
counterattack of enemy penetrations;
relief operations;
composition of a highly mobile reserve; and
support for LRRP and special operations.

While glamorous and flashy, helicopters were viewed by the Army as just another means of transport, and were employed to enhance the ground combat mission. The fundamental concept of airmobility was that Army aircraft increased the ground combat force's capability to perform, and provided a better balance among the five fundamentals of combat: mobility, firepower, intelligence, command and control, and communications. Aviation units were allocated to support ground units as missions required. In addition to combat units, combat support and service support units had to be airmobile as well if adequate support was to be put on the ground.

The most common type of airmobile mission in Vietnam was the delivery of ground troops into an area of operations (AO) – a combat assault. To execute such an operation required much more than merely loading troops onto choppers and flying them into a jungle clearing; it involved a great deal of coordination between numerous units and commands.

Airmobility provided ground forces with the mobility and support to seize terrain, envelop enemy dispositions, deprive the enemy of required resources, divert his attention, and destroy his forces. The airmobile assault supported all types of offensive operations: movement to contact, reconnaissance-in-force, raids, limited-objective attacks, coordinated attacks, exploitation and pursuit. The airmobile assault force could get into an area quickly, assault deeply into enemy territory, and by-pass intervening enemy forces and rough terrain. It allowed the frontal attack to be avoided, and provided the ability rapidly to reinforce successful attacks and to resupply engaged forces.

By definition, the typical airmobile assault was essentially a movement-to-contact. The ground force was moved to an area by helicopters and inserted in enemy territory, and thereafter moved by foot to engage him. The enemy was usually encountered in a meeting engagement. The force seizing the initiative in a meeting engagement has the advantage; airmobility enhanced the capacity of the friendly force to achieve this, because of its ability to move rapidly, by-pass rough terrain, reinforce or reposition units, and resupply them. Blocking forces could also be inserted to engage withdrawing enemy (the pursuit mission).

A reserve was essential to reinforce, exploit success, or attack from another direction; reserve and reaction forces were usually kept on "strip alert," with helicopters on stand-by for immediate commitment. Companies and even platoons were leap-frogged around the AO by helicopter in efforts to make contact with the elusive enemy – these were called "Jitterbug" operations. Many such techniques were employed. The Marines used four UH-34s carrying ARVN troops on airborne stand-by for "Chickenhawk" operations, to be inserted to intercept withdrawing VC flushed out by ground operations.

## Planning an airmobile assault

The planners of an airmobile assault first considered the mission and objectives of the ground force. The plan for the ground operation was based on intelligence of enemy locations and activities. Owing to the vastness of the AO, the rugged and concealing terrain and the nature of the enemy, it was extremely difficult to locate him. He had no frontlines, rear area logistics or support units. The enemy was mobile, and deployed widely dispersed

A Pathfinder (distinguishable by his authorized camouflage clothing) operating as a forward air controller at a unit base, using the same AN/PRC-25 radio as rifle companies – though Pathfinders were provided with headsets and voice-operated microphones to allow hands-free operation. He stands beside a helicopter pen constructed of sandbags reveted with airfield matting and U-section barbed wire pickets, both painted olive drab. (Leroy "Red" Wilson)

November 1966: carrying ammo and rations, a Marine UH-34D Seahorse is directed to land at a 3d MarDiv hilltop outpost near Hue/Phu Bai. Eyes were often painted on the noses of helicopters, though usually giving a fiercer appearance than this rather dopey-looking example. (US Marine Corps, courtesy Simon Dunstan)

until concentrating immediately before an action. He devoted a great deal of skilful effort to remaining concealed, presented only a fleeting signature, and required minimal logistical support. This made it difficult for Free World forces to find, fix and destroy him.

The ground operation plan considered possible enemy strength, deployment and armament; the civilian situation in the area (enemy-controlled/sympathetic and friendly villages), LZs, ground movement routes, weather, terrain obstacles, proximity to major enemy base areas and favored sanctuaries (Cambodia, Laos), and the distance from helicopter refueling and rearming points.

The AO was first reconnoitered by map, aerial photography and visual reconnaissance over-flights. The latter would be conducted by the ground and aviation commanders and the artillery liaison. Time permitting, air cavalry units might be employed, sometimes inserting aero rifle platoon patrols, LRRP teams and airdropped motion-sensors. Nevertheless, the amount of air activity over a future AO had to be limited so as not to alert the enemy; airmobile operations required surprise, and this could not be sacrificed. Detailed reconnaissance and extensive preparations compromised some operations: once they were executed, the AO was often found empty – the alerted enemy was seldom found waiting in ambush. The artillery preparation could warn the enemy as well. Limiting the reconnaissance and circumventing artillery prep was risky, but could yield good results by catching the enemy unprepared.

Units operated only under an umbrella of artillery firing from firebases.[9] To provide more and better fire support, additional temporary firebases might be established around the AO. Air Force close air support (CAS) would be coordinated, as would airborne forward air controllers (FAC) and psychological operations aircraft. Medevac units and field hospitals would be put on stand-by, ammunition resupply loads assembled on heliports, and the various ground units alerted. The ground and aviation units would often have to be pre-positioned prior to launching the operation; reserves and reaction forces were designated and pre-positioned. Helicopter refueling and rearming points had to be stocked; pallets of ammunition and 500-gal rubber fuel bladders ("elephant turds") would be sling-loaded into firebases selected for this purpose.

Larger operations could be quite complex, involving two or three infantry battalions or more, ground and air reconnaissance units, artillery, several aviation units, Air Force elements, and other Free World forces. Coordination had to be affected between all of these organizations, with approval granted by higher commands and Vietnamese authorities. Airspace coordination was critical to prevent

9 See Fortress 58, *Vietnam Fire Support Bases.*

mid-air collisions and danger from artillery fires; altitude separation was established between the different air routes and in the zone of action. Time schedules were worked out, in the full knowledge that once the operation commenced changes would be inevitable and constant.

The lift units were normally notified the day before the operation, usually by 1800 hours (6pm), but in an emergency or to exploit a contact as little as one hour's notice might be given. Lift units had to assign the available aircraft and crews; fuel and ammo-up the aircraft; determine the number of lifts required; coordinate with gunship escorts (a problem greatly eased when assault companies had organic gunships); determine flight times; plan flight routes and altitudes; specify flight and landing formations, and direction of approach; obtain and assess the weather forecast; and coordinate with scout elements. They needed to be apprised of the fire support plan, and the radio frequencies and callsigns of all involved units. (Aviation units retained their callsigns for the duration of their service in Vietnam; while in conventional wars this was considered a serious violation of signal security, it was not a major factor in Vietnam. Frequencies were often changed only monthly).

A reverse planning schedule was developed, to determine the time spans necessary to conduct mission preparations, fly to the PZ, load the troops, fly them to the LZ, and return to the PZ to conduct subsequent lifts. Planners also had to factor in how many lifts could be made before refueling was necessary, and the flight times to bases for refueling – these might be other than the lift unit's base. Different routes were used to and from the LZ; when multiple lifts were made, the in-and-out routes were slightly altered so that they would not fly over the same areas twice. The approach into and out of the LZ would also be varied, although this was not always possible in tall jungle and in mountainous areas. When multiple lifts were required, subsequent lifts might be shifted to another LZ.

October 1969: a "Loach" from 101st AbnDiv (AmbI) lands on a temporary pad at an FSB. The preliminary gathering of intelligence by every means available was vital to the success of an airmobile assault, to include visual observation at very low level by the OH-6As of the aero scout White platoons. (US Army, courtesy Simon Dunstan)

## Landing zones

The selection of LZs was critical. In a search-and-clear operation several LZs would be selected, in order to insert companies and battalions in favorable areas from which to launch the ground phase. Alternate LZs were designated for use if enemy action or terrain conditions made the primary LZs unusable. Because of the scarcity of LZs in many areas, the locations of those few that were available often dictated the ground plan. Additional LZs would be selected for insertion of troops in later phases, for blocking positions, and for resupply and medevac.

While airmobile operation plans had to support the ground operation, the LZs – the points where the assault force transitioned from a helicopter-delivered "cargo" into a ground assault force – often effected the ground plan. The proximity of LZs to suspected enemy locations was important. The surprise of a sudden airmobile assault might be wasted by choice of a too-distant LZ that required too long for the ground force to reach the objective, especially if intervening natural obstacles or broken terrain exhausted the troops. The alerted enemy might thus be allowed time to withdraw, or to counterattack the assault force.

In Vietnam's rougher terrain the choice of LZs was sometimes limited by dense forests, swamps, broken ground, mountains, hills and ravines. In other areas – the plateaux of the Central Highlands, some inland coastal areas, and the Mekong Delta – potential LZs were plentiful. In areas where LZs were scarce the problem was compounded by the ease with which the enemy could keep potential LZs under surveillance or establish ambushes. If desperately needed for LZs, semi-clear areas – with small numbers of scattered trees devoid of underbrush – might be clear-cut. This required engineers with a security team to be inserted by rappeling, or moving by foot from a more distant LZ, and to clear the trees with demolitions and chainsaws; although this would negate the element of surprise, it was sometimes unavoidable. Only one or two helicopters could land on such LZs. "One-ship" LZs often had to be cleared by ground troops for medevacs and resupply. Sometimes a ridge crest clear of vegetation could be used for a precarious helicopter landing.

Roads and intersections, if sufficiently clear of adjacent trees, might be used, as might sandbars and broad sand flats inside river bends. Land-clearing companies using large bulldozers cleared the sides of main roads out to 100–500 meters, as well as cutting wide lanes through forests as an aid to detecting enemy movement from the air. Both the bulldozers and the areas they cleared were called "Rome plows" (after the company producing the dozer blades), and such areas could be used as LZs.

Attempts were made to blast LZs with 1,000lb bombs; but this required numerous bombs, and their accuracy was not such that multiple hits would be sufficiently close to provide a usable clearing – which in any case would be cratered and littered with tree trunks and limbs. "Arc Light" strips – the codename for B-52 bomber strikes – were swathes blasted through the forest, and could be hundreds of meters across and 1–3km long. While the trees were flattened, such strikes created a nightmare for infantrymen to cross, with large craters and masses of shattered and uprooted trees; after any length of time these tangled obstacles were made worse by rapidly growing tropical vegetation. From late 1968 use was made of 10,000lb M121 and, from

A jungle landing zone blasted by a 10,000lb M121 demolition bomb; it is large enough for a single Huey, and a squad of engineers with chainsaws and demolition charges can enlarge it into a two-ship LZ within an hour. With a light bulldozer delivered by a CH-54 "Flying Crane" it could be cleared into a larger LZ, or even enlarged to take a howitzer battery firebase, in one day.

1970, 15,000lb BLU-82 bombs dropped from CH-54 Flying Cranes and Air Force C-130 transports (the "Commando Vault" Program) to blast LZs. Detonating 3ft above ground, these munitions produced no craters, disintegrated trees within about a 40–50 meter diameter, and sheered off trees for another hundred meters.

A single helicopter required an area of between 20 and 75 meters diameter to land, depending on the model. Dust, sand and vegetation debris thrown up by the rotor-wash could blind pilots, causing them to become disoriented and lose visual contact with the ground, other helicopters and nearby obstacles. Gravel, small rocks, dirt clods, tree limbs and other debris could damage rotor blades and engine turbines, and could also be blown into other helicopters. Rocks, tree stumps, deep mud, high grass and dense brush on LZs prevented helicopters from setting down. Rocks, stumps and fallen trees could damage the landing gear or the bottom of the fuselage, and landing gear could become stuck in thick mud. Rotor-wash only flattened the grass out like a mat, hiding obstructions and, in the rainy season, flooded areas.

To avoid these hazards, helicopters would not land, but would hover as low as possible to discharge troops. This was dangerous for the troops: hidden obstructions could injure them, and they might be jumping into deep mud or water – not a place to be if the enemy opened fire. Elephant grass was extremely dense and could be anything from 2ft to 8ft tall; this was a considerable drop for a combat-loaded infantryman, and presented a genuine danger of injury.

If the ground sloped at less than a 7 percent gradient, the helicopter landed with the nose oriented up-slope; if it was between 7 and 15 percent, it landed side-slope. If the slope was greater than 15 percent a helicopter could not land, owing to the danger of blade-strike on the high side, and instead would hover to discharge its troops. It was desirable to land and take off into the wind; however, if the tactical situation, the need to make maximum use of available landing space, or obstacles on the approach so dictated, then helicopters could land in crosswinds of up to 10 knots or tailwinds of up to 5 knots. This varied between aircraft types, the larger machines being better able to handle cross- and tailwinds. However, when in contact with the enemy these restrictions were ignored unless winds were excessive.

The altitude of the LZ, high temperatures and humidity all affected the "allowable cargo load" that could be carried. A helicopter taking off with a heavy load on the coastal plain might not be able to land in a high mountain area. While helicopters are known for their ability to hover, land and take off vertically, they might not be able to do so with a heavy load when landing at high elevations or under poor air-density conditions. Loaded helicopters then needed to make low-angle approaches not unlike those of a fixed-wing plane, although once off-loaded they could take off vertically if conditions were right. This often prevented loaded helicopters from landing vertically into small tree-ringed clearings; an empty chopper might have been able to do so, but then its load would be extremely limited for take-off.

## THE AIRMOBILE ASSAULT

### The pick-up

The units to be lifted were not too concerned about the air movement plan. They were merely being delivered; they were mostly concerned with their own actions once on the ground. The ground units might be picked up at a single point or from multiple PZs. This pick-up zone might be a firebase, a brigade or division base, or a clearing in the jungle where they were already conducting an operation.

The unit would break down into "sticks" according to the number of aircraft and the lift restrictions imposed by air-density and altitude. This, coupled with the attachment of extra personnel, meant that squad integrity could seldom be maintained. Excess squad members who

Pick-up: sticks from Co A, 1-503d Inf, 173d Abn Bde, photographed in dried-out rice paddies on May 17, 1966, as the Hueys come in to load them at a PZ northwest of Vung Tau on the coast of III CTZ, southeast of Saigon. In the foreground are a mortar squad with the baseplate, tube and bipod of an 81mm M29A1; weight restrictions dictated that only a small number of mortar rounds could be carried for an airmobile assault. (US Army, courtesy Simon Dunstan)

could not be loaded on the same chopper with their squads were simply collected together in additional sticks and landed by later lifts. This was far from ideal, for obvious reasons, but it could not be helped. Many opposed it because of the consequent lack of unit integrity and command and control if the LZ proved "hot." Headquarters and support elements would be split between different helicopters, "cross-loaded" to prevent their complete loss if a chopper was downed. A platoon leader, platoon sergeant or squad leader would be on each chopper to maintain control on the ground. If the unit was engaged immediately upon insertion it would fight as "sticks" until the arrival of the rest of the unit enabled it to consolidate.

Troops loading onto choppers were to approach from the nose, thus giving the pilots a clear view of them. It was not uncommon to approach from one side, with half of the troops rounding the nose to load on the other side. It was essential that the tail rotor be avoided. If conducting a "hot" or "engine-running" on-load – as most were – soft caps were removed and radio antennas secured and bent to prevent blade-strikes. If troop seats were installed the men took them, but they often did not use seatbelts because of their burdensome web gear and rucksacks. They were just as likely to sit on the floor; removing seats reduced weight, provided more space, and allowed rapid boarding and off-loading. Aircrews were nervous about armed troops carrying grenades. Weapons were locked and loaded, but set on safe. Weapons were supposed to be carried muzzle-down so an accidental discharge would do little damage. The crew chief supervised loading, and relayed communications between the aircraft commander and troop leader. Last minute situation changes would be relayed by the C&C chopper to all the helicopters, then on to the troop leader in each chopper from the aircraft commander via the crew chief.

Landing: a smoke screen laid by a chopper partly masks an LZ in ricefields near Trang Bang on September 25, 1968, as a "Vee" formation of five UH-1Ds from 116th Assault Helicopter Company begins to land troops from 4–9th Inf, 25th Division. Note the pale effect of the rotor-wash flattening the vegetation. This LZ is large enough for many more choppers to land, but no more than six at a time went in; this minimized the number of aircraft for control purposes, and reduced the chance of collisions. Whenever possible the Hueys maintained the same formation during the flight and the landing, to simplify planning, coordination and control. (US Army, courtesy Simon Dunstan)

## The approach flight

The flight formation might be an arrowhead (the most common), a diamond, echeloned (staggered 45 degrees right or left of the line of flight), a trail (column), or a staggered trail. The flight would land in the same formation, and this was dictated by the shape and size of the LZ and the ground unit's deployment plan. Escorting gunships would fly on the flanks, usually one per side. If there were more gunships, they would follow the formation; and two others might be tasked with flying ahead and prepping the LZ. Gunships, because of their ammunition loads, carried limited fuel and could only remain on station for a short time; follow-on flights of gunships would relieve those on-station, although there might be gaps in coverage.

There were usually insufficient helicopters to move the unit in a single lift, or else the LZ was too small for the unit to be inserted simultaneously. Multiple "serials" – or unofficially, "lifts" – were organized, based on the number of helicopters and the size of the LZ. A unit might be inserted on two or more LZs in the same area if available; this allowed more of the force to be landed at once, and provided dispersal. This latter aspect was not always desirable, however, as it could cause serious problems if scattered ground units became engaged and were unable to support one another; it could also make it difficult to coordinate artillery and aerial fire support.

To insert a 100-man rifle company (full strength was about 160 men, but companies could number as few as 80) required 15 UH-1Hs with a load limit of seven troops each. Only eight to ten helicopters might be provided, however, and the problem could be complicated by the LZ's being able to accept only four choppers at once. In this case the serials would be subdivided into "flights" of the number of helicopters the LZ could accept (a flight was two or more aircraft, a serial was two or more flights). Flights could arrive at intervals of as little as 15 to 30 seconds; this was all the time necessary to off-load and depart. Even on large LZs able to accept an entire serial, the four or five helicopters lifting each rifle platoon might land in phased sequence rather than all at once, so as to avoid major losses if ambushed.

## Preparation fires

The artillery preparation usually lasted ten minutes or less, and was placed along the treelines and on suspected enemy locations, especially on any dominating ground. The artillery "fire fan" had to be taken into account when selecting the aviation approach route; while there were rare instances of helicopters being downed by an errant artillery round, most units put their faith in the "big sky, little bullet" theory. Artillery was timed so that the last rounds impacted when the lift was two minutes out, and the last two rounds were white phosphorus, the smoke providing the signal that the barrage had ended. Any ARA gunships prepping the LZ now dashed ahead and blasted the treeline in their turn. They would pull out of their run as the troop-carrying "slicks" came over the trees, and then orbit on call. The escorts on either side of the formation would make a firing run along the treelines as the slicks landed; they would then break into a "racetrack" – an oval flight pattern – and wait to pick up the flight as it departed the LZ again, taking up stations on either flank.

## Off-loading

The troops would be alerted when on the final approach. The whole process became routine for an infantryman after he had gone through it once or twice.[10] The troops disembarked on order of the crew chief, whether the chopper was actually on the ground or hovering a few feet above it; if hovering, they would swing their legs over the side and step off the skid. (The earlier choppers had a troop door on the right side only, which impeded deployment. Larger helicopters like the CH-47 and CH-46 were loaded and unloaded via the tailgate ramp.) If taken under fire, the troops knew not to fire from inside the chopper even if the door gunners opened fire. This prevented dismounting troops and nearby helicopters from being hit. If fire was received before any troops dismounted, the flight commander might cancel the landing. More often, the troops would go out anyway; it was an unwritten rule that if even one man off-loaded and the enemy opened fire, then everyone followed. Hot LZs were the exception rather than the rule.

Normally the troops off-loaded from both sides and would clear away from the chopper until it lifted off. They would then move off the LZ as rapidly as possible and assemble on its edge. Once everyone was accounted for, squads would move to establish a perimeter. If engaged

Off-loading: Operation "Oregon," Quang Ngai province, April 24, 1967. These troopers jumping from a hovering UH-1D are from the Blue aero rifle platoon of Troop B, 1–9th Cavalry, 1st CavDiv (Airmobile). The slick is named "Darlin' Jenny II," indicating that the commander had previously lost a bird; naming of aircraft was encouraged, as good for morale. (US Army, courtesy Simon Dunstan)

[10] See Warrior 98, *US Army Infantryman in Vietnam 1965–73.*

on the LZ the initial small force could be in for a vicious fight. The enemy, if present in force and determined to fight, would make every effort to overrun them or at least inflict serious casualties before the next lift arrived. They knew the air assault force would immediately call for attack helicopters, artillery, and CAS. Such a fight could turn into a slugging match, and escalate into a major battle. On the other hand, the enemy might just as likely break contact.

### Command and control
During the course of the operation a battalion C&C chopper orbited high overhead. This aircraft, supplied by the brigade aviation section or the general aviation company, carried the commander of the ground unit to which the assault units belonged – for example, the brigade commander if one or more of his battalions was being inserted, and even a C&C from division. The battalion commander of the unit being inserted would also be airborne, controlling and coordinating the many moving parts of the operation; he would be accompanied by the S3 (operations) officer and artillery and aviation liaison officers.

This system was often criticized, on the grounds that the commander might lose his "feel for the ground" – i.e. lose touch with the ground time-distance factor, leading him to expect his company commanders to cover ground more rapidly than was realistic. From the air, distances seemed inconsequential; the aerial observer could not appreciate the difficulty of broken terrain hidden by trees and other vegetation, and might forget the weight of the loads his men were carrying and the temperature and humidity on the ground.

Nevertheless, for those commanders who could retain a realistic perspective it was a better place to be for command and control purposes, rather than struggling through dense brush unable to see further than 10 or 20 meters. Units on the ground could mark their position with radioed encoded grid coordinates, colored smoke grenades, pop-up flares fired through the forest canopy, marker panels and signal mirrors, so a commander's assistant could plot friendly

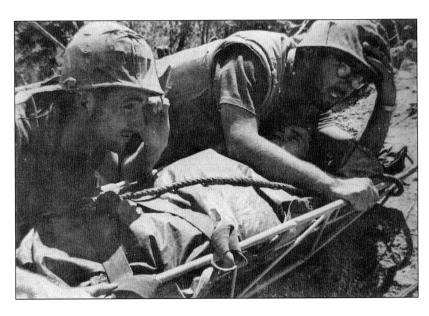

Medevac: Marines shelter a wounded comrade, lashed into a gray-painted Stokes litter, from the considerable rotor-wash and debris of a Dust-Off chopper.

locations and enemy sightings on a map board. Artillery, gunships, scout helicopters, CAS, medevacs, resupply, and commitment of reserves and reaction forces were all coordinated from an aerial vantage point, with a very quick response time.

## Reinforcement, medevac and resupply

As subsequent lifts arrived the combat power built up. Scout choppers were scouring the surrounding area for enemy withdrawing or moving toward the LZ, and gunships were on call. Often the LZ served only as a point of delivery, and once the entire unit had arrived they moved out on their mission. In other instances, however, a ground command post was established, mortars were set up or even artillery flown in, and the LZ might be used as a base of operations for sweeps into the surrounding area. Resupply lifts would be flown in, while at least one company secured the LZ. Follow-on companies and support, to include mortars and artillery, would be flown in by CH-47s or (if Marines) CH-53s.

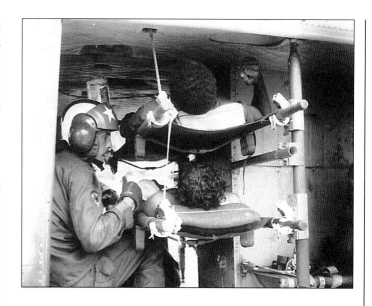

June 24, 1971, FSB Mace: aboard a chopper of "Long Binh Dust-off," an SP5 medic of 45th Med Co (Helicopter Ambulance) – with his helmet painted in the red, white and blue of the Texas flag – cares for two men wounded by mortar fragments. The unarmed medevac Hueys could carry up to six litter cases. (US Army, courtesy Simon Dunstan)

From the first moments of the assault the medevac choppers were on call to lift casualties out, and the "Dust-Off" crews were renowned for their willingness to extract casualties from PZs under intense fire. Theirs was a more dangerous job than the assault slicks, who often managed to slip in and out without opposition. Once the ground unit was engaged and casualties had to be extracted the Dust-Offs could be guaranteed a hot reception, and their red cross markings gave them no protection at all.

Units would spend days and weeks on the ground, and relied totally on helicopter resupply. Typically, units would receive a "light resup" every three days; this usually consisted only of rations ("rats"), radio batteries ("bats") and water. Critical replacement items might be delivered, and sick and non-combat minor injured flown out. Every sixth day brought a "major resup"; this was sometimes a rest day, or at least part of one. Units would move to and secure a small LZ, sometimes hacking it out of a semi-clear area. More rats, bats and water were delivered along with mail, and mail carried out. Worn-out uniforms were replaced; damaged or malfunctioning weapons and equipment would be "direct exchanged" (DXed). Replacement troops might be delivered, as well as men returning from R&R and recovered sick and wounded. Men whose tours were up or who were due for R&R were given a lift out. Two or three flights might arrive during such a day.

The work of assault helicopter companies was endless. Emergency ammunition and water resupply was delivered when units were in contact; this might simply involve throwing the boxes and water cans out while hovering over low trees. Rather than waiting for medevacs, wounded and prisoners might be taken out by the resupply bird. Firebases were almost totally resupplied and supported by helicopters.

# GUNSHIP TACTICS

Attack helicopters included the UH-1B/C gunships, Aerial Rocket Artillery UH-1Bs, and AH-1 Cobras. Their armament varied widely, even between examples of the same models. The UH-1B/C gunships were gradually replaced by the Cobra, whose speed and maneuverability made it much more capable. The ARA aircraft were purely rocket-firers, lacking forward-firing machine guns and grenade-launchers; they delivered only aerial fire support, augmenting or sometimes substituting for field artillery, and technically they were not gunships.

Attack helicopters supporting airmobile units performed three types of missions: escort and reconnaissance, direct aerial fire support, and security. These missions might be performed concurrently. Escort and reconnaissance, usually referred to simply as "escort," entailed accompanying troop lift flights, engaging antiaircraft weapons encountered en route, scouting the LZ and placing preparatory fire on it, and direct fire support if the ground force was engaged. Direct aerial fire support took the form of both on-call and preplanned missions in support of ground units, including firebases and other installations, which came under attack. In this role gunship fires augmented but did not replace field artillery, mortars, and close air support by "fast movers." As with those fire support systems, any soldier could call for and direct gunships; they could support units at any echelon from a battalion to a six-man LRRP team, but the type of ordnance carried by gunships had a major effect on their capabilities. Security missions involved scouting for enemy activity in the vicinity of bases, and escorting ground convoys.

The escort mission was usually performed by the assault helicopter company's organic aerial weapons platoon, or the battalion's aerial weapons company; direct fire support missions were usually conducted by air cavalry troops. These latter missions usually involved the gunships working directly with LOHs. A "light fire team," usually one gunship and one LOH, was the most common element, though in some units that term was used for a pair of gunships. A "heavy fire team" was two gunships and one LOH. A pure gunship team was often called a Red Team, while a mixed team was a Pink Team — a mix of Red Platoon gunships and White Platoon scouts. Gunships were never employed singly; they were always accompanied by either a "Loach" or another gunship.

### Ground/air communications and fire control

When a ground unit in contact with the enemy requested gunship support, a light fire team was usually dispatched; gunship and air cavalry units maintained elements on alert 24 hours a day. En route

This UH-1B ARA ship mounts the 24-tube 2.75in M3 armament subsystem, along with a 40mm M75 automatic grenade launcher in an M5 chin turret – the latter was not often fitted to ARA Hueys. This aircraft is in Stateside glossy dark OD finish with full-color markings.

An AH-1G Cobra gunship of an air cavalry troop – note the red-over-white guidon painted below the rotor. On this example the chin turret, tailboom horizontal stabilizers and the heel of the vertical stabilizer are painted red, identifying the troop's aero weapons "Red Platoon." The buzz number "648" has been overpainted yellow for quick identification.

the team leader would contact the ground unit on its frequency, giving his callsign, the type of fire team, and his estimated time of arrival. The ground unit would provide the grid coordinates of the target, the distance in meters and direction to the target from the ground unit's location (this might be given as a cardinal direction or in degrees). If they were within 600 meters of the enemy – and it was seldom that they were not – the ground unit would declare "Danger Close." Gunship fire could be brought in to less than 100 meters from friendly troops, but it was a dangerous proposition; firing rockets, in particular, was avoided within 200 meters of friendlies. The ground unit would also notify the team leader of any artillery, mortars and CAS being employed, and provide their callsigns and frequencies. They would also warn of any antiaircraft fire. All helicopters in the team monitored the radio traffic, but only the team leader communicated with the ground commander, in order to avoid confusion.

It was essential that the friendly unit's location be determined in relation to the target. Colored smoke grenades were the most common means of doing this. Red smoke signified a unit in contact or warned of danger; white was used for target marking or reference points; and violet or yellow marked friendly unit locations. Green smoke was seldom used, since it was difficult to distinguish against vegetation, though it could be used in areas of bleached-out dried growth. If possible the unit marked the center of its position and its flanks, but sometimes the situation was too chaotic to do this. Standard procedure was for the unit to "pop smoke" and alert the fire team that it had done so; the fire team would not be told the color, but would identify it once sighted. The enemy sometimes monitored friendly radio traffic, and might attempt to pop smoke of the same color to confuse aviators.

A prominent terrain feature, identifiable from the air, might be designated as a reference point for the fire team to orient on the target – for instance, a distinctive hilltop, a road junction or a pond; in jungle terrain and on the plains such features were often too widely dispersed to use effectively. The fire team might either drop a white smoke grenade or fire a WP rocket for a reference point, or might simply use the unit's marking smoke. The ground unit could also mark the target area using M79 HE grenades or smoke rounds and tracer fire.

A "sharkmouth" AH-1G from Troop D, 3d Sqn, 4th Cavalry of the 25th InfDiv returns to its base at Cu Chi after a mission during the April–June 1970 Cambodia invasion. (US Army, courtesy Simon Dunstan)

Unless high hills dictated the direction of approach, the gunships would make their runs from a direction at right-angles to the unit's front line; if at all possible they would avoid over-flying or firing over the unit's position. The ground unit had a better view of the target, and could more easily assess the effects of aerial fire and adjust it. Unlike standard operating procedure for artillery or mortar fire, no attempt was made to "bracket" the target; this wasted ordnance and fuel, and exposed gunships to more ground fire. Once the first run had been made the impact area usually became the reference point for subsequent runs. The goal was to adjust the second strike directly onto the target. Corrections were given in meters, using one of three methods: target location – from a reference point using cardinal directions and degrees in azimuth (direction); round impact – cardinal direction and distance in relation to the target; and observer-target line – left, right, add, drop the distance from the observer to the target. Once the fire fell on or very close to the target, any final small corrections were transmitted and the ground commander directed, "Fire for effect."

The high volume of machine gun, grenade-launcher and rocket fire was quite destructive and much feared by the VC/NVA. It was not uncommon for enemy units to attempt to disengage when they heard the gunships approaching, or soon after the first strikes were delivered. However, a larger and better prepared unit might slug it out. Ever since facing the limited and poorly controlled air support available to the French Army in the 1950s, they had learned the value of moving in as close as possible and "hugging" the Free World unit, to frustrate attempts to bring them under fire from the air. Accepting the risks of "friendly fire" hits, ground units often brought in gunship fire "right on top" of their own positions.

Scout helicopters usually operated in conjunction with gunships, detecting targets and directing fire. Scouts sometimes went in ahead of gunships to look for signs of enemy activity around LZs, and to draw fire; the gunships might remain out of sight until the scout had stirred things up. It was seldom that a VC would be so foolish as to fire on a passing Cobra that did not appear to be on an attack run. LOHs would often get down among the trees, and in open areas might hover just a few feet off the ground where they could actually see footprints in the dirt. If engaged, the scout would return fire if possible, but it was more likely to dart out of the area and call in the "guns." LOHs were also used for visual reconnaissance (VR) missions, providing unit commanders with the opportunity to observe their future LZs and surrounding ground. This was extremely valuable; maps offered only so much detail, and VR allowed detection of many small terrain features and obstacles – inundated ground, swamps, and especially dense underbrush – before boots were put on the ground.

# ASSESSMENT OF OPERATIONS

There was not a ground operation conducted in Vietnam that was not supported by helicopters, whether the infantry were airmobile or not. Some operations, such as the defense of Khe Sanh and its subsequent relief, relied so heavily upon helicopters that they could not have been conducted without them.[11] Ground operations relied on all aspects and capabilities of helicopters – mobility, reconnaissance, security, combat and administrative transport, fire support, logistics, command and control, and medical evacuation. It was not only airmobile divisions that enjoyed these capabilities – a fact that led some to question the need for dedicated airmobile formations. However, the airmobile division's capabilities and efficiency were greatly enhanced by the habitual assignment of particular aviation units. This provided for solid command relationships, and gave commanders the ability to rapidly mass aviation assets and employ them as necessary without the delays that would be caused by requesting and coordinating them through non-divisional channels.

For effective operations, not every division needed to possess this capability. An airmobile division provided a theater commander with a strong, highly agile, responsive asset capable of a wide range of missions. It could operate over a larger area than other divisions, making it ideal for counterinsurgency operations, area control, flank security, deep attacks (given limited enemy air defenses and friendly air superiority), and economy-of-force missions. In Vietnam the airmobile units were used as "fire brigades," able to deploy rapidly to other parts of the country and to effect control over wide areas.

There were attendant problems, such as the massive maintenance and logistics demands of helicopters, their vulnerability to fire and sensitivity to weather, and the lengthy training time required of air and maintenance crews. The detractors of airmobility cite these problems,

[11] See Campaign 150, *Khe Sanh 1967–68*

Carrying 3,000lb loads of ammunition in sling nets, Marine CH-46A Sea Knights of HMM-364, based at Phu Bai, rush in to resupply Hill 881S west of Khe Sanh, which was held by the 3–26th Marines during the siege of January–April 1968. This was a "Super Gaggle" mission, consisting of eight to 16 "Phrogs" escorted by up to a dozen Marine A-4 Skyhawk jets and four UH-1E gunships. The A-4s would attack known and suspected gun positions in the vicinity of the outpost with napalm and tear-gas spray; two laid smoke screens on either side of the approach seconds before the helicopters roared in, while four continued to hit suspected positions as the CH-46s dropped their loads and were out again in a matter of seconds. (US Marine Corps, courtesy Simon Dunstan)

and claim that the US placed too much reliance on the helicopter in Vietnam; but any system or concept has its limitations, which have to be taken into account.

The conduct of sustained oper-ations to the extent achieved by the US could not have been accomplished with only a small number of helicopters. Without the massive investment in helicopters and all the personnel and resources needed to deploy and sustain them, units would only have been able to stay on the ground for about six days before returning to base for resupply. The ability to insert ground forces anywhere and at any time would have been lost, as would the ability to by-pass restrictive terrain. The ability to emplace and sustain the bases themselves would not have existed without extensive helicopter support. Aerial reconnaissance was a primary means of finding and fixing the enemy, as was the insertion and extraction of reconnaissance teams. Reliable medevac was responsible for saving countless lives, and was of major importance to morale. While first considered new, innovative, and even romantic, airmobility proved itself in a most challenging combat environment, and was accepted as an essential capability.

* * *

The 1st CavDiv left Vietnam in April 1971; its 3d Bde remained until June 1972. Deployed to Ft Hood, TX, the division was reorganized as an experimental "Triple-Capability" (TRICAP) division, with airmobile, mechanized and tank battalions. The mobility differential, and uneven ability of the dissimilar brigades to take and hold ground, proved unworkable. It was soon reorganized as an armored division, and remains so today.

The 101st AbnDiv remained in Vietnam until March 1972, when it returned to Ft Campbell, KY. It was redesignated 101st AbnDiv (Air Assault) in October 1974, and remains today the Army's only airmobile division. The division or elements have since served in the Gulf War, Rwanda, Somalia, Haiti, Bosnia, Iran and Afghanistan, where it made good use of its airmobility.

The restructuring of the Army after Vietnam saw an increase in aviation units throughout, but companies were reduced in size. Divisional aviation battalions were eventually enlarged to brigades, and new types of units were created. Among these was the 6th Cavalry Bde (Air Combat), an airmobile antiarmor force. New helicopters, with advanced capabilities that could only have been dreamed of in Vietnam, were fielded.

The Marines, too, fully realized the value of their air assault capabilities, and placed more emphasis on the development and employment of such units. They recognized the insufficiency of their attack and light transport helicopter units, and these were increased. A new balance of medium and heavy helicopter squadrons was achieved, changing from three-to-one to two-to-one.

There can be little doubt that the successes of airmobility in Vietnam demonstrated its value to the full spectrum of combat capabilities. While Vietnam is considered by some today as a dark spot in the history of the US armed forces, it cannot be denied that the impact it had on the military use of helicopters was extraordinary and long-lasting.

# FURTHER READING

Butterworth, W.E., *Flying Army: The Modern Air Arm of the US Army* (Doubleday, 1971)

Carland, John M., *How We Got There: Air Assault Warfare and the Emergence of the 1st Cavalry Division (Airmobile) 1950–1965* (Institute of Land Warfare, 2003)

Cheng, Christopher C.S., *Air Mobility: the Development of a Doctrine* (Praeger, 1994)

Chinnery, Philip D., *Vietnam: The Helicopter War* (Naval Institute Press, 1991)

Fails, William R., *Marines and Helicopters 1962–1973* (Headquarters, Marine Corps, 1978)

Galvin, John R., *Air Assault: The Development of Airmobile Warfare* (Hawthorn Books, 1969)

Halberstadt, Hans, *Army Aviation* (Presidio Press, 1990)

Mesko, Jim, *Airmobile: the Helicopter War in Vietnam* (Squadron/Signal Publications, 1984)

Moore, Harold G., & Joseph L.Galloway, *We Were Soldiers Once… and Young: Ia Drang – The Battle That Changed the War in Vietnam* (Harper, 1993)

Stanton, Shelby L., *The 1st Cav in Vietnam: Anatomy of a Division* (Presidio Press, 1987 – originally titled *Anatomy of a Division*)

Stanton, Shelby L., *The Rise and Fall of an American Army: US Ground Forces in Vietnam, 1965–1973* (Presidio Press, 1985)

Stanton, Shelby L., *Vietnam Order of Battle: A Complete Illustrated Reference to US Army Combat and Support Forces in Vietnam 1961–1973* (Stackpole Books, 2003)

Tolson, John J., *Airmobility 1961–1971* (Vietnam Studies; US Army, 1973)

Williams, Dr James W., *A History of Army Aviation: From Its Beginnings to the War on Terror* (Lincoln, NE: iUniverse, 2005 – e-book available on-line)

Young, Ralph B., *Army Aviation in Vietnam: An Illustrated History of Unit Insignia, Aircraft Camouflage & Markings, Vol 1 & 2* (Huey Company, 1999 & 2000)


US Army, *Aviation Battalion, Group, and Brigade*, FM 1–15 (December 1969)

US Army, *Army Aviation Utilization*, FM 1–100 (August 1969 & October 1971)

US Army, *Airmobile Operations*, FM 57–35 (October 1967 & March 1971)

US Army, *Pathfinder Operations*, FM 57–38 (October 1968)

(These and other manuals are available from Military/Info Publishing: http://www.military-info.com/Index.htm.)

# PLATE COMMENTARIES

## A: AIRCRAFT RECOVERY, AND EARLY HELICOPTERS
### A1: CH-37B Mojave
### A2: CH-21C Shawnee

The recovery of downed helicopters was crucial – they were expensive. Helicopters going down in enemy-controlled areas were first stripped of their weapons, ammunition, radios, avionics, and such items as maps and signal operating instructions (containing radio frequencies, callsigns, code-words, etc). If the situation did not permit this, then the downed chopper would be destroyed by aerial rocket fire. However, the vast majority of helicopters could be recovered and either repaired, rebuilt, or cannibalized for replacement parts – for which the demand in combat zones was insatiable. A heavy lift helicopter was necessary to recover damaged choppers. The wreck's rotors first had to be removed, and – depending upon the type of lift aircraft available and

November 1967: while the door gunner holds his M60D pointing at the dirt for safety, men from 3d Bn, 12th Infantry, 4th InfDiv jump from a hovering UH-1D during the fighting near Dak To. The hilltop has been blasted by artillery – note the torn appearance of the tree stump and fallen trunks. The light construction of the Huey, and the underfloor position of the fuel tank, discouraged actual landings among these kinds of obstacles. (US Army, courtesy Simon Dunstan)

the helicopter to be recovered – the engines might also have to be lifted out separately.

Initially the Army and Marines used the CH-37B Mojave (prior to 1962, HR2S-1), but this type was retired in 1965, to be replaced by the Army's CH-47 Chinook and CH-54 Tarhe "Skycrane", and in the Marine Corps by the CH-53 Sea Stallion. The first troop lift helicopter to see wide use in Vietnam, operated in support of the ARVN by US Army light aviation companies from the end of 1961, was the CH-21C Shawnee – "Flying Banana" or "Hog Two-One". It began to be phased out in favor of the UH-1 "Huey" series in 1963, but remained in use into the following year.

## B: TROOP LIFT
### B1: UH-1D Iroquois
### B2: UH-1C Iroquois
Of all the many and varied missions that helicopters performed in Vietnam the most important was moving troops, and this was the primary mission of the Huey. Here a UH-1D "slick" off-loads infantrymen while still in a hover. This technique was advantageous for the helicopter and crew, because it prevented damage from stumps and rocks hidden by vegetation, and the possible detonation of mines or booby-traps on the LZ, and also allowed a more rapid lift-off if taken under fire; however, it increased the chances of ankle and knee injuries among the heavily loaded troops. While the Huey was rated to carry 11 infantrymen each weighing 240lb including their equipment (109kg – 17 stone), the typical limit

in Vietnam was six or seven men. Usually the chopper's troop seats and soundproofing insulation were removed to save weight; removing seats also allowed troops to embark and off-load quickly, and prevented the snagging of their equipment in the seat webbing. Initially the side doors were retained, to be closed at higher altitudes, but later they were removed altogether to save weight.

The door gunners would normally spray the treeline during the final approach to the LZ, taking extra care to be aware of the location of other choppers. The passengers were cautioned not to fire from the door even if they saw a target. The door gunner would cease fire as the infantrymen were about to off-load.

In the background, a UH-1C "Hog" gunship, fitted with the XM-200 pod for 19x 17lb 2.75in FFARs, circles after "prepping" the treeline immediately before the troop landing.

## C: AERIAL FIRE SUPPORT
### C1: AH-1G Huey Cobra
### C2: OH-6A Cayuse
Fire support – delivered with 2.75in rockets, 7.62mm machine guns and 40mm automatic grenade-launchers – was invaluable to ground units. Before mid-1967 gunship support was provided by UH-1B or -1C "Hogs"; at that time the first dedicated attack helicopter, the AH-1G or "Snake," began to arrive in-country. They were operated by air cavalry troops, which were organized into Red, White and Blue platoons – respectively, aero weapons, with gunships; aero scouts; and aero rifle, the ground scouts with their Huey lift choppers. Here a light observation team or "Pink Team" – that is, a combination of a Red gunship and a White scout – are in action. The crew of the OH-6A "Loach" have visually reconnoitered a suspected area and have spotted enemy activity or drawn fire; the observer has dropped a red smoke grenade to mark the target, and the pilot wheels away as the gunship makes its run. If necessary the scout will further adjust the Cobra's fire by signaling corrections in relation to the smoke grenade.

## D & E: CONDUCT OF AN AIRMOBILE ASSAULT
An airmobile assault was a complex operation involving many "moving pieces," all of which had to be coordinated and timed in detail. This operation – the insertion of a rifle company – is somewhat simplified; the operation would actually have begun the previous day, when the mission was requested, the various aviation units were tasked, and the orders for other support assets were coordinated.

**D1:** The landing zone has been selected, based on the mission and objective of the rifle company.
**D2:** A temporary fire support base is established on a hilltop, and its fires are coordinated with other artillery fire bases.
**D3:** OH-6 scout helicopters from an air cavalry troop reconnoiter the LZ and the surrounding area.
**D4:** Artillery preparation begins shortly before the "lift birds" arrive.
**D5:** A UH-1 command-and-control chopper arrives on station, and serves to control air traffic and fire support.
**D6:** Immediately ahead of the lift, AH-1 gunships "prep" the LZ with machine gun, rocket and grenade-launcher fire.

**E1:** A low-flying UH-1 lays a smoke screen along the treeline.
**E2:** The first troop lift of UH-1 "slicks" arrives.
**E3:** Two further lifts will be needed to deliver the whole company.

**E4:** An air cavalry heavy fire team – 2x AH-1s and an OH-6 – orbits some distance away, ready to be called in for support if necessary.

**E5:** Air Force F-4 Phantom fighter-bombers suppress nearby possible enemy positions with napalm, and remain on call to deliver CAS for the inserted company.

**E6:** An Air Force forward air controller in a 0-1 Birddog directs the fighter-bombers, and coordinates with the ground and air commanders.

**E7:** An on-call UH-1 medevac chopper orbits, awaiting calls for Dust-Off; others are on "strip alert."

## F: ARTILLERY RAID
### F1: CH-47A Chinook
### F2: M102 105mm howitzer

The 1st CavDiv developed the artillery raid technique to capitalize on its airmobility. Based on intelligence provided by air cavalry scouts, LRRPs, aerial photography and civilian information, enemy targets within a particular area were selected. Artillery raids were often planned and executed in less than three hours, making them highly responsive to emerging intelligence. Several firing positions were selected on hilltops, and rifle platoons were inserted by helicopter to secure them; if necessary, engineers would blast and chainsaw trees to clear the site. Within minutes, two or four guns with their crews and ammunition were delivered to each position and set up, and opened fire on multiple targets in the area. The use of several sites simultaneously prevented some targets from being masked by high ground, and targets could be attacked from several directions. After less than half an hour the Chinooks would extract the guns and displace them to other firing positions. The raids were conducted so rapidly that they kept the enemy off-balance and uncertain as to when and where they would occur, and denied him the time to mount attacks on the firing positions.

(In reality, this scene would be masked by much more blowing dust and debris from the Chinook's rotor-wash.)

## G: MARINE AIR ASSAULT
### G1: CH-53A Sea Stallion
### G2: CH-46D Sea Knight
### G3: M274 Mechanical Mule

The Marine Corps' vertical envelopment concept was an extension of the amphibious assault. The aerial assault was envisaged as being made well behind the landing beach,

and potentially "hot" LZs were to be avoided. Larger capacity helicopters were employed, so as to put as many troops and their heavy weapons on the ground as rapidly as possible. The CH-46A Sea Knight was the primary troop-lifter; it could carry 17 combat-loaded Marines – considerably more than the Army's UH-1D/H with its maximum of 11 men. This was fortunate; the Marines used a 14-man squad organization, in place of the 11-man Army squad, and even operating under climate-induced load restrictions the CH-46A could still usually carry a full squad. Alternatively it could carry half-ton M274 Mechanical Mule weapons carriers internally, or sling-load a 105mm M101A1 howitzer. In 1966 the CH-46D was introduced, with more powerful engines and capable of carrying 25 troops. Here a Mule mounting a 106mm M40A1 recoilless rifle has been debarked from a CH-46D; this weapon could fire HEAT and WP rounds to 1,200 meters. The Mule could also transport the 81mm M29 mortar.

The CH-53A Sea Stallion, introduced in 1966 to replace the CH-37B Mojave, was the Corps' heavy lifter. This "Super Bird" or "Buff" could carry up to 53 combat-equipped troops, or could sling-load a 155mm M114A1 howitzer or an M50A1 Ontos tracked antitank vehicle mounting six 106mm recoilless rifles.

## H: LAM SON 719 – LARGE SCALE AIRMOBILE OFFENSIVE

This map shows one of the largest ARVN and US airmobile operations conducted during the war. Its objective was to neutralize the extensive NVA logistics bases around Tchepone in southern Laos. The ARVN 1st InfDiv, AbnDiv, 1st Armor Bde and 1st Ranger Group attacked into Laos on January 30, 1971. While ground forces advanced into Laos, most of the units were delivered, supported and supplied by helicopter; scores of US aviation units were concentrated under the direct command of the 101st AbnDiv (Airmobile). Artillery and logistical support was also provided by the US, but US ground forces did not cross the border. NVA air defenses were the heaviest encountered during the war – 19 antiaircraft battalions – and by the time the operation ceased on March 24, 106 US helicopters had been destroyed and 618 damaged; US aircrew losses were 65 dead, 42 missing and 818 wounded. The ARVN were forced to withdraw by determined NVA counterattacks, including the unexpected use of armor. The results of the operation may be described as mixed.

A downed AH-1G Cobra, with a suitable marking on the nose; even though it was totally destroyed, the two crewmen survived. More than twice as fast as the overburdened UH-1C "Hog," and with potentially three times the loiter time over target, the AH-1G was still far from invulnerable to enemy fire. It had only light armor for the engine, fuel and hydraulic systems, and only the bottom part of the fuel tank was self-sealing (a feature that other helicopters lacked altogether). The Cobra's cockpit was hot and uncomfortable, since – unlike a Huey's – it was totally enclosed, while not providing any protection against the sun; cockpit temperature could easily exceed 100 degrees Fahrenheit. (Leroy "Red" Wilson)

# INDEX